WE ONLY DATED FOR 11 INSTAGRAMS

AND OTHER THINGS YOU'LL OVERHEAR IN L.A.

RUNNING PRESS

PHILADELPHIA

For Charlie, who never stopped believing in me.

Special thanks to Beverly, Matthew, James, Ned, Mercedes, Steve, Loeb, Emmet, Jon, Bridget, and Fabrice.

Copyright © 2018 by Jesse Margolis
Cover illustration copyright © 2018 by Yoko Honda
Interior illustrations copyright © 2018 by Emmet Truxes

Running Press
Hachette Book Group
1290 Avenue of the Americas, New York, NY 10104
www.runningpress.com
@Running_Press

Printed in Canada

First Edition: October 2018

Published by Running Press, an imprint of Perseus Books, LLC, a subsidiary of Hachette Book Group, Inc. The Running Press name and logo is a trademark of the Hachette Book Group.

The Hachette Speakers Bureau provides a wide range of authors for speaking events. To find out more, go to www.hachettespeakersbureau.com or call (866) 376-6591.

The publisher is not responsible for websites (or their content) that are not owned by the publisher.

Print book cover and interior design by Amanda Richmond.

Library of Congress Control Number: 2018938590

ISBNs: 978-0-7624-6463-0 (hardcover), 978-0-7624-6462-3 (ebook)

FRI

10 9 8 7 6 5 4 3 2

Contents

Foreword

A Hollywood historian once told me that during the Golden Age of Hollywood, the Brown Derby was the preferred restaurant of gossip columnists because its circular shape allowed strategically placed patrons to overhear the conversations of studio executives and movie stars.

We've been overhearing each other ever since in a city that is like no other. Los Angeles is the most diverse city in human history, with more than 220 languages and dialects spoken—and overheard—across our 500 square miles. Of course, we are still home to Hollywood, one of America's greatest exports. But we also have a tech industry that's taken hold in Silicon Beach and beyond, as well as aerospace, architecture, fashion, green technology, and many more cutting-edge business pursuits that weave together our curiosity and creativity.

This is a place where our boulevards aren't just streets, they are iconic landmarks immortalized by our greatest musicians and filmmakers. Our mountains and hills aren't just for hiking, they are dotted with homes made famous by pioneering photographers. The weather isn't just great, it's a foundation for our California state of mind. When you are here, in this City of Angels, it's hard to escape the feeling that you can think and talk about anything—that anything is possible. There is no city that embodies global progress and culture quite like L.A.

What truly makes Los Angeles a special place is our four million people. Together they make our city a snapshot today of what America will be tomorrow—a city where diversity doesn't pull us apart but brings us together. This is a town where everyone can find a place to belong, to raise a family, or to start a business. Yes, we have our quirks, those little things you can't fully understand unless you live here—but doesn't any great city?

Every Angeleno can tell you their surefire workaround to the 405. We all have our favorite taco guy, which can spark some pretty fierce debates. We all have our reactions to a celebrity sighting and opinions on whether you should be a USC or a UCLA fan. We have our juice cleanses, our aura screenings, and our pet spas. And if there's one thing I've learned from reading @OverheardLA, it's that dating in this city can be quite the adventure. But there's no better place to fall in love.

It's that collective spirit of Angelenos—all of our glory and peculiarities—that @OverheardLA captures so well.

What excites me about this book is that it not only embodies the strengths and intelligence of our residents but also highlights our ability to laugh at ourselves. It captures the urban, tech-savvy, global perspective of our millennial Angelenos as they move through the trials and tribulations of early adulthood.

These pages are filled with material that is at once "so L.A." but also a reflection of the fact that here in Los Angeles, the global is local and the local is global. We are all a part of this shared culture. The artists, creators, laborers, and countless others who fill these pages not only represent L.A. but the entire world around us.

With that, I invite you to come visit our Pacific paradise—both in the pages of this book and in person. Come experience and overhear our world, and you might never want to leave.

–Eric Garcetti,
42nd mayor of Los Angeles, Overheard superfan

#Intro[*]

Writing a book using other people's words . . .

The @OverheardLA account started virtually by accident, after I happened to catch bits of an annoying conversation playing out between two women at Erewhon (a high-end supermarket and bad sitcom pilot waiting to happen). They were talking about everything from vegans to pit bulls to the intricacies of egg freezing, but mostly they were complaining about their friend Lisa who was obsessed with "Scchhhwwaaaaagg." Over the course of the next week, I posted some of the gems from their conversation on my otherwise horrible private account. Not long after, a screenwriter friend (Allan Loeb, averages 18,000 steps a day) and a songwriter friend (James Webber, roving genius) convinced me to start an account called @OverheardLA, dedicated to entertaining snippets I was lucky enough to overhear.

Obviously, the concept of publishing overheard conversations has been around for a while, but something about the combination of Los Angeles absurdity, the social media revolution, and Instagram's visual platform made the idea feel worthwhile. Plus, I was bored, hated my job, and was crying out for some type of creative expression (one day, the world will see the horrible emoji book covers and latte Rorschach tests that were the prelude to Overheard).

[*] If you have opened this book, PLEASE close it. Nobody reads anymore. Please photograph the cover, tag us and your friends, and put it on the upcycled nightstand you stupidly dragged home from the flea market last year.

Boring story short, I created the account and came up with a few basic rules:

1. No photos.

2. You should never be able to identify somebody by reading a quote.

3. Comedy over gossip. No mentioning of individuals (this rule has been broken a few times, but only because Brendan Fraser was making a comeback and the world needed to know).

4. Never make the account about me. It's about the city. Nothing is worse than these Instagrammers who "come out" and try to be wannabe celebrities. You know who I'm talking about.

The account immediately resonated, probably because in addition to the intrinsic absurdity of this wonderful city, many people saw a small part of themselves in the content. You may not think you're "L.A.," but very few people are immune to the charms and misdemeanors of the city's culture.

Eight months after launching the account, I was sitting in Verve "working" when two girls sat next to me at the counter. The following is a paraphrased account of their conversation.

"So, what's your writing process?"
"It could be anything. Like, have you heard of this Instagram @Overheard LA? It's fucking stupid. Not all the posts are, but some are. Sometimes I'll read their stuff and get inspired. There was a post about someone who wears glitter to the gym. So I was like maybe I'll write a song about glitter."

It was then that I began praying daily . . . that I would turn on the radio one day and hear a song about glitter.

Four months later I met my friend and collaborator, an Ivy League genius/architect/cartoonist named Emmet. His account, @brooklyncartoons, is like the millennial version of the great *New Yorker* cartoons. We decided to do a book together... even though no one reads books, which is why I'm on Instagram in the first place. Fuck, this was a huge mistake.

A week before turning in this manuscript to my publisher, something incredible happened. I was at a coffee shop in Silver Lake, meeting with a friend. We were discussing the subject of dating, one of the "dark topics" of Los Angeles (along with global warming, the tangerine barbarian in the White House, and stomach issues). I half-jokingly said something that boomeranged back to me six hours later as a DM submission on Overheard. I swear I'd noticed this little artsy girl darting her eyes, listening, and judging the conversation, but I had no idea she would fulfill my two-year dream of being "overheard."

> "I just want to meet a cute, normal girl. Someone who hasn't fucked [talented celebrity name removed], [#MeToo-accused celebrity name removed], [terrible actor celebrity name removed], or the other nine guys every girl has hooked up with in L.A."

In this poetic full-circle moment, I realized none of us is immune to our own ridiculousness.

In closing, I want to say thank you to everyone who supports and contributes to the Overheard accounts. Unfortunately, the brilliant monsters who created social media couldn't come up with a better word than "followers." We are honored to have your attention and support, even if it's just for 6 seconds a day. @OverheardLA is only possible because of the unique, self-aware community of Angelenos who send in sound bites from the cafes, hiking trails, nightclubs, and tantric sound baths around town.

To all the actors, doctors, writers, firefighters, bloggers, assistants, cacao shamans, real estate agents, bartenders, Uber drivers, cult leaders, uninfluential influencers, models turned nutritionists, yoga teachers, real teachers, augmented reality development executives, and "creative directors" . . . a sincere thank-you.

Jesse Margolis,
creator of Overheard

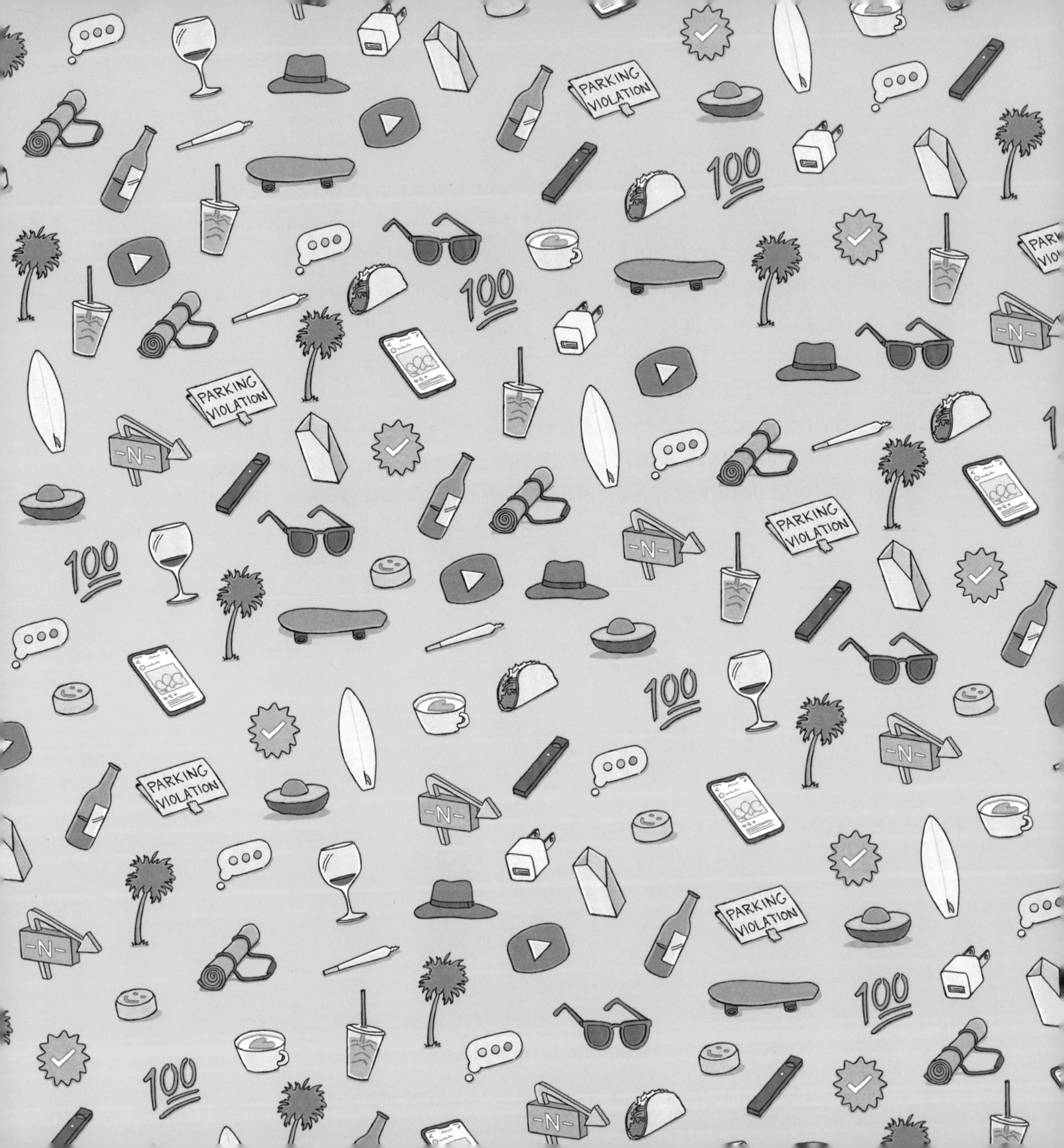
PARKING VIOLATION
100
-N-

#DATING

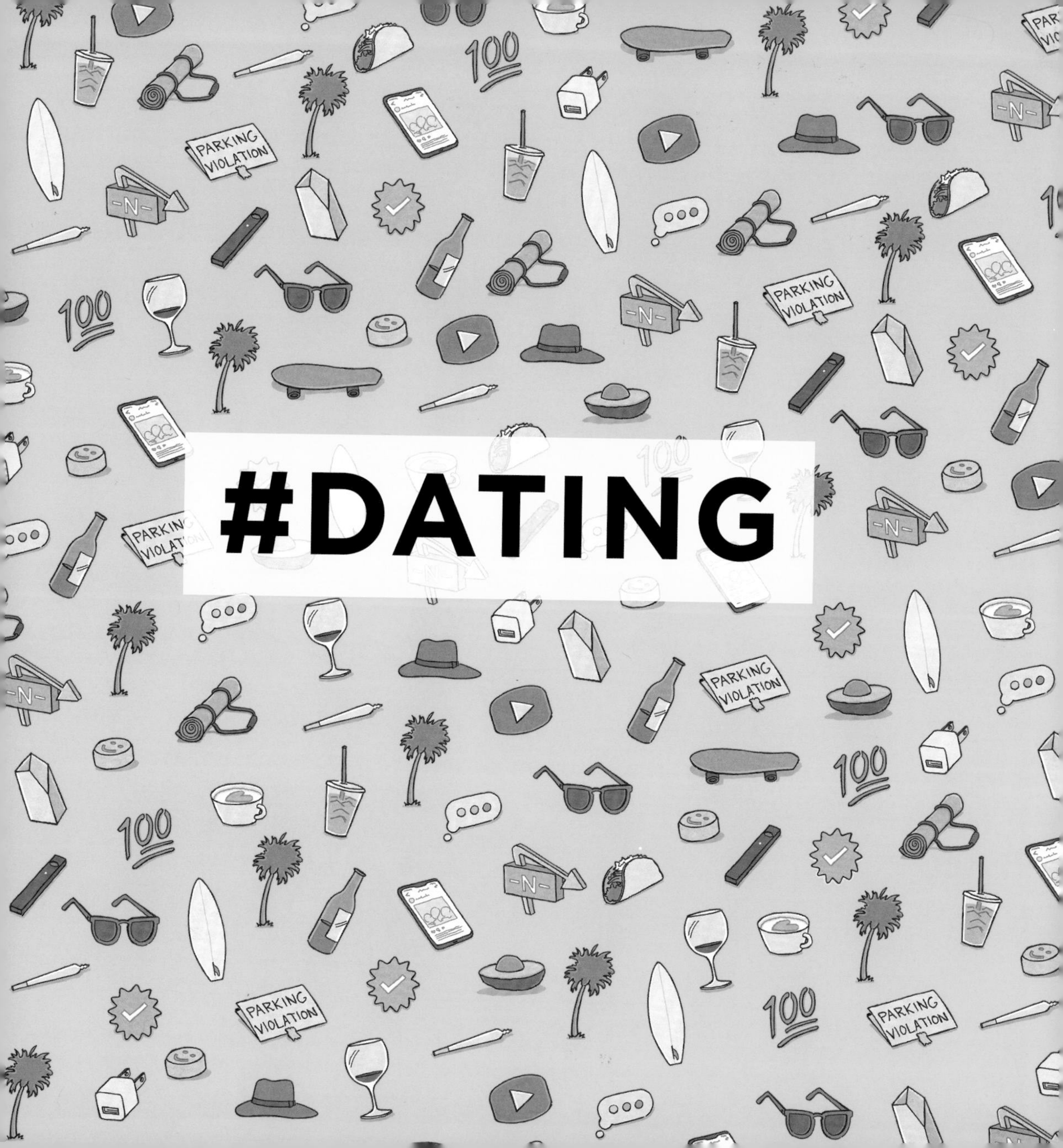
PARKING VIOLATION
100

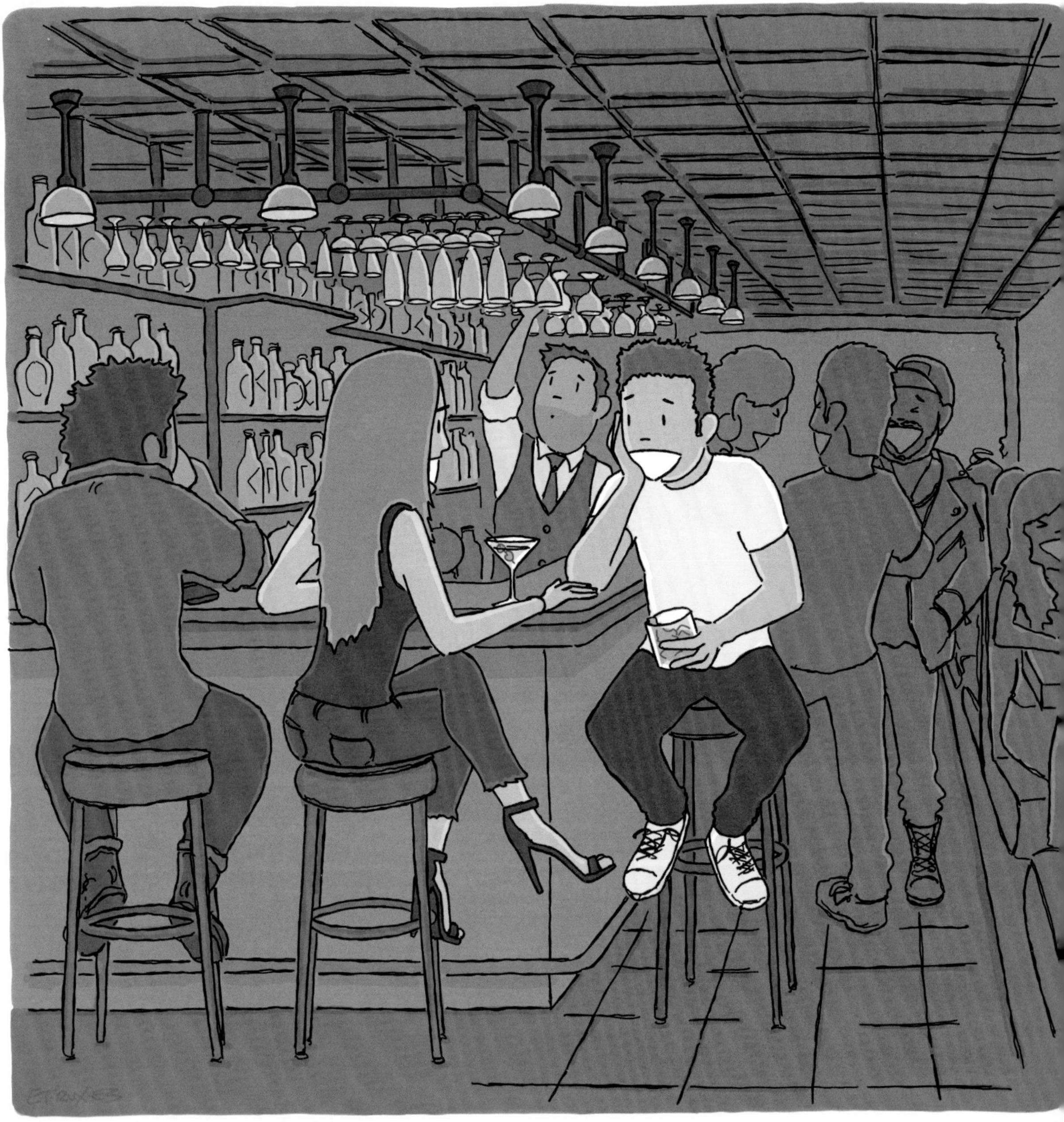

Guy and Girl on date:
"I want to go viral with you."

"I'd like that."

"He's 31, but like North Carolina 31, like, two kids and a mortgage. 31-year-old dudes in Los Angeles are just learning how to cook a fucking chicken."

Umami Burger. Cahuenga Blvd.

#NC31 #LA31

"Every psycho I've ever dated was a Leo."

"Every psycho I've ever dated believed in astrology."

"He told me he deleted his Bumble app."

"So basically he said, 'I love you.'"

"Instead of bringing flowers, he brought me vitamins. He said they were like 'roses for my immune system.'"

Erewhon Market.
**Find a guy who takes you to a gluten-free yoga class in a cold-pressed oxygen chamber and then surprises you with Paleo stevia chocolates and raw camel milk from Morocco.
#vitaman #LoveInTheTimeOfHollywood

"He added me on Snapchat so I added him on LinkedIn to business-zone him . . . that's even worse than the friend zone, by the way."

Sweetfin Poké. Santa Monica.

#BusinessZone

"Don't waste your tears on that boy. L.A. is a desert; you need to stay hydrated."

Wurstkuche. Venice.

#WaterIsLife

Girl 1: Go on a date . . . let him in.

Girl 2: Let him in? I don't even let cars in on the 101!

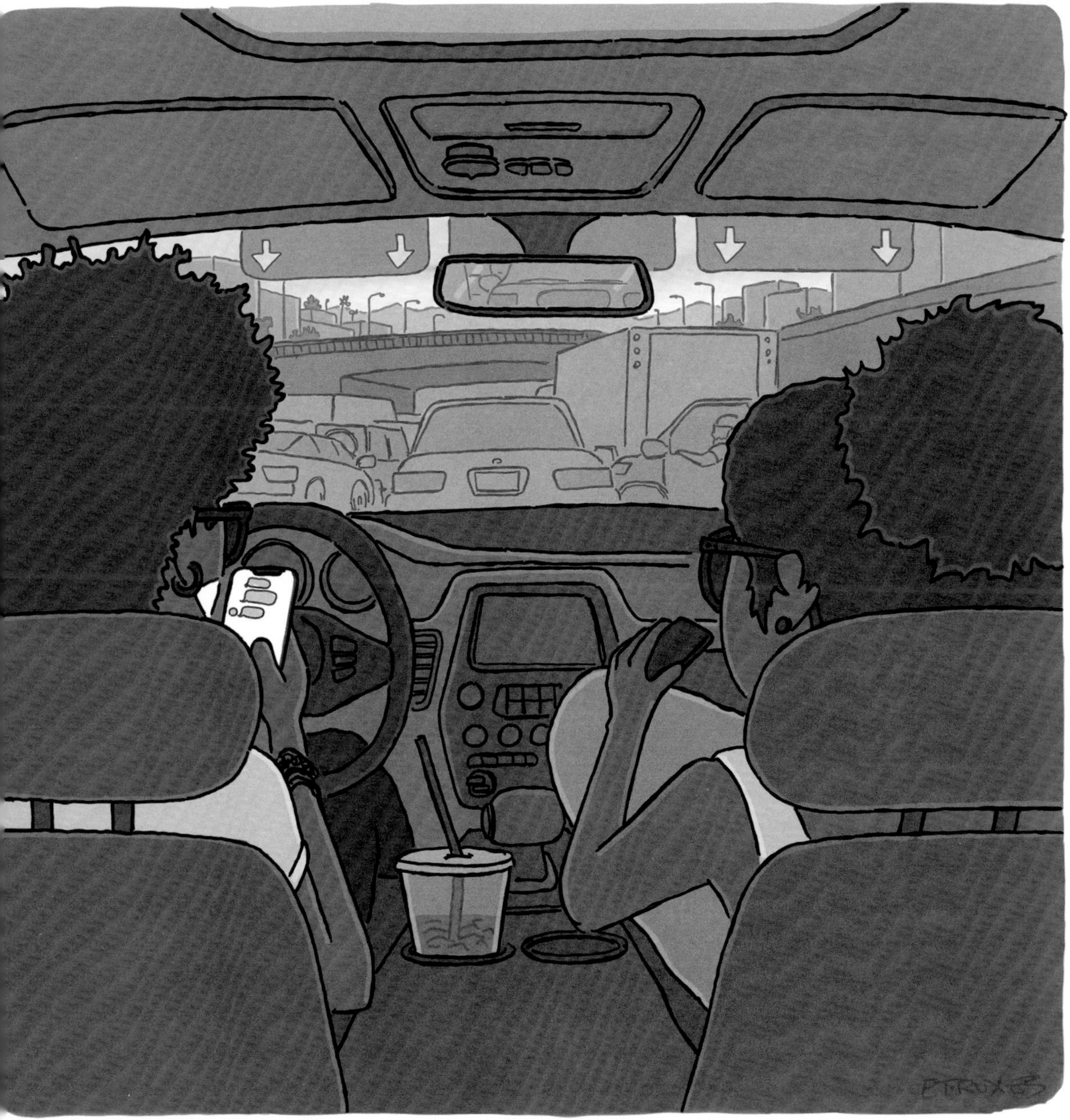

"I'm dating three girls and it's destroying my stomach."

"Why?"

"One is vegan, one is paleo, and the other eats KFC."

Laurel Hardware.

#DietaryThreesome

"Dating is so expensive . . .
It's like two beers and one Uber
surge and I can't eat for a week."

U-Zen. West L.A.

**Money can't buy you love, but it can buy you grass-fed burgers
and artisanal beers and the chance to get to know your work
crush McKenna, and potentially make out with her in an Uber X
while the driver plays System of a Down and blathers on about
his screenplay, "Ass Gun."

#LoveAndMoney #mckenna

"We're not exclusive, but we have a really long Snap streak, which is basically the highest form of millennial commitment."

Alfred Coffee. Brentwood.

#streaking

"When did we meet?"

"Fuck if I know, check our DMs."

Little Dom's. Los Feliz.

#OriginStory

"We had another fight. She got crazy drunk, and as I was leaving she screamed '*Avada Kedavra*!'"

Tattle Tale Room. Culver City.

#WANDerlust #CurseWords

"You just know he has an STD."

"How do you know that?!"

"Well . . . his name is Chad."

Urth Caffe. DTLA.
#CertainlyHasADisease

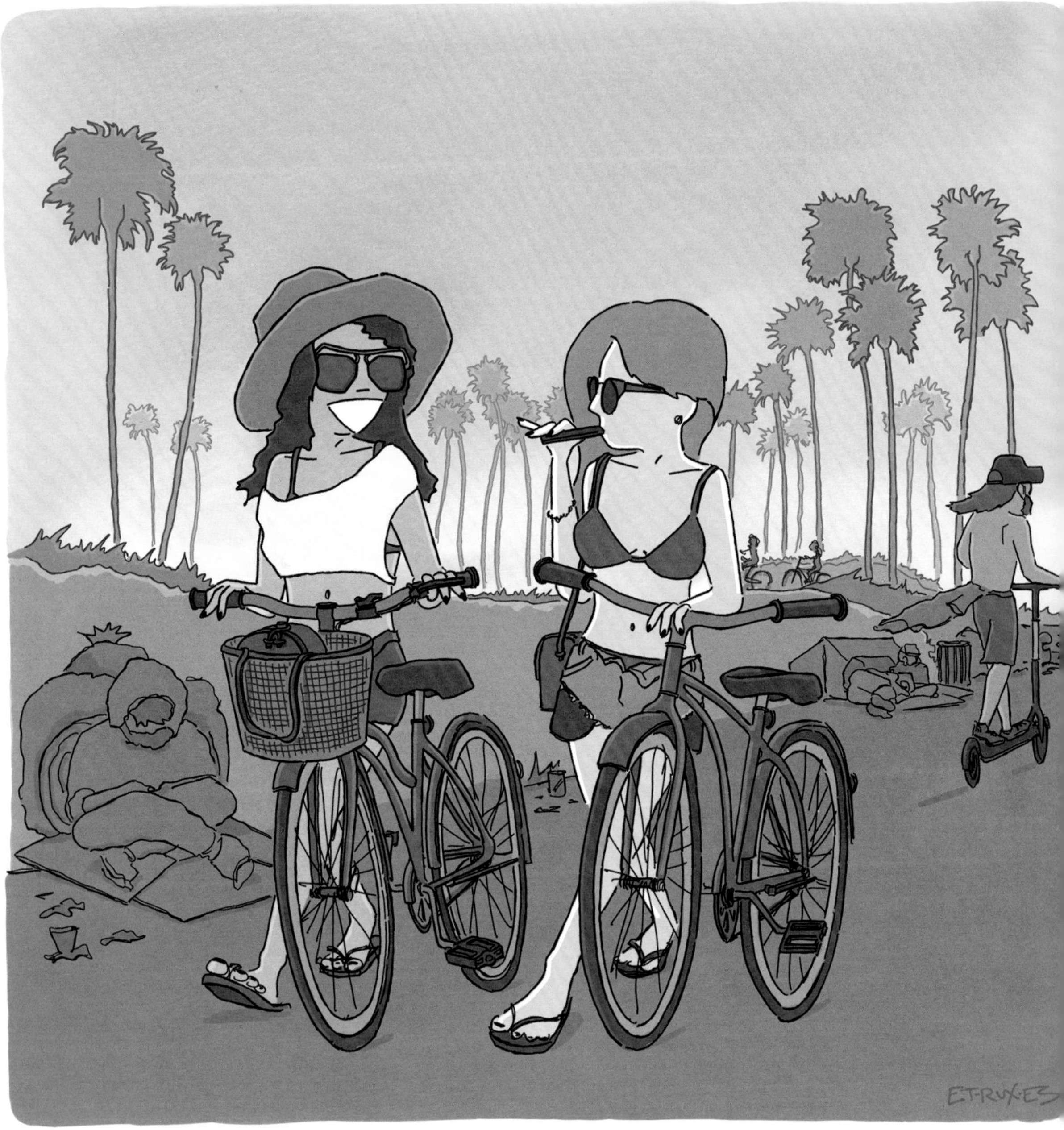

"I'm not a slut. I just have
a lot of soul mates."

"I can't believe he bought you a flight."

"It's the new drink."

Republique.
**If he's buying you flights, there is a 90% chance he is a trust fund monster who copies and pastes bad quips he got from his 'dating guru' and DMs 112 girls a day. Pay for your own trips, and let him pay for the really ridiculous shit, like a drone that brings you organic camel milk every morning."
#clouddigger #CamelMilkLatte

"I realize we're on a date right now so this might sound kinda weird, but I'm not really into dating."

Sugarfish. La Brea.

#AnInconvenientTruth

"I can't date him, his name is too weird."

"What do you mean? His name is Carl."

"No. His dad is Carl. He's Carl Jr."

Lukshon. Culver City.
#miniburger

Uber driver to passenger:
"My girl dragged me to see that big Christmas tree at the Grove. I was like 10 seconds from dumping her, but then I realized that shit is magical. Somehow I wound up agreeing to take her on a cruise to Cabo for New Year's."

101 South.
#LoveBoat

"My phone is a cemetery. Just
the ghosts of texts unanswered."

LACMA.

#poltertexts #ModernDayRilke

"He was trying to fuck me all morning. But in a really respectful way."

Tavern. Brentwood.

#AlarmCock

"Timing is everything, whether it's love, sex, or avocados."

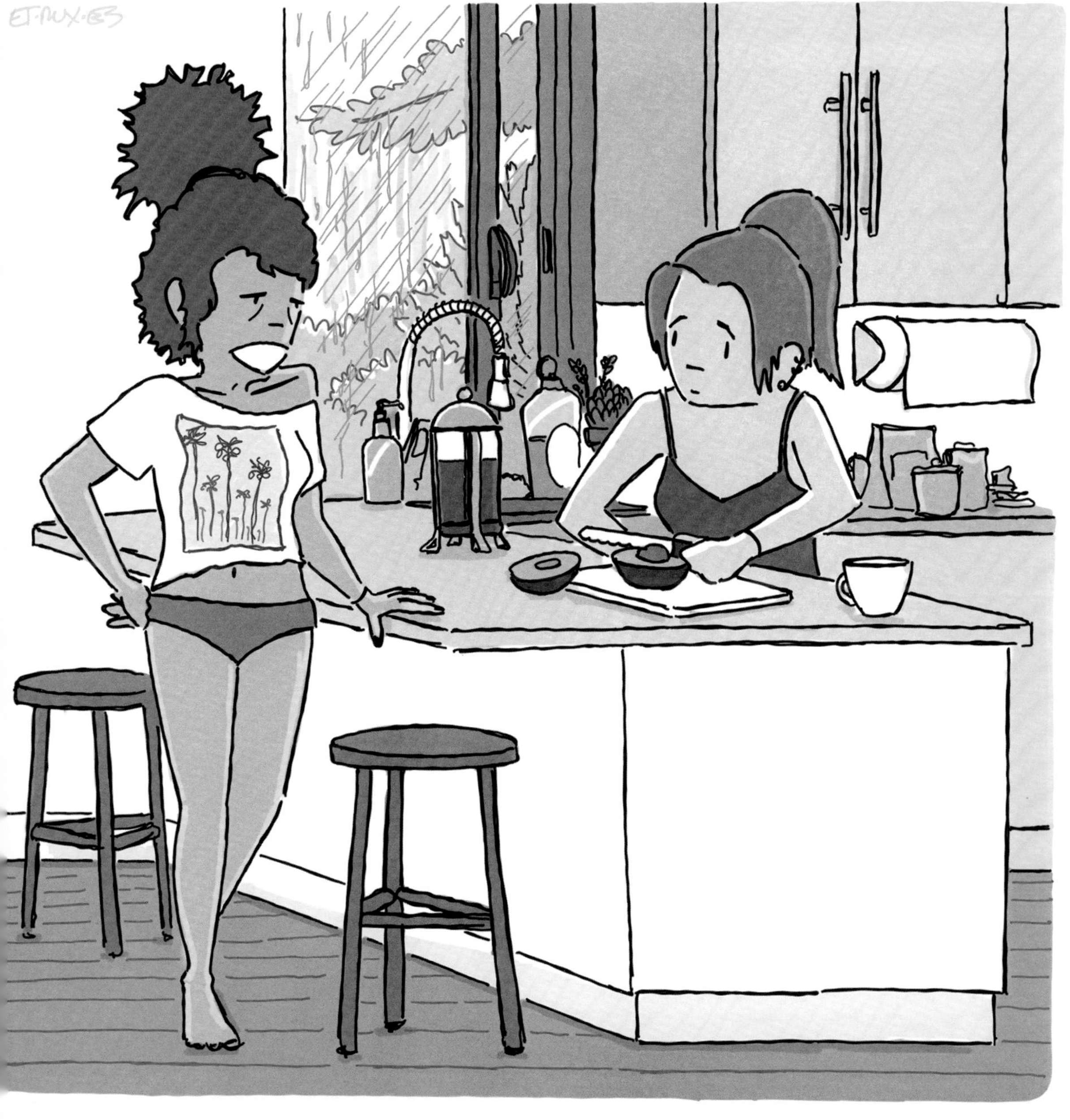

"Remember when you listened to that Cat Power song for two weeks straight because a cute plus-sized model didn't text you back and we all thought you were gay?"

Dinner Party. Marina Del Rey.

#CATastrophe

"Of all the girls currently ghosting me right now, she's definitely the coolest."

Abbott Kinney Blvd. Venice.

#FriendlyGhost

"My sugar daddy broke his leg water skiing and forgot to wire me money for the month. I feel awkward asking him, so I emailed his brother."

Blind Dragon.
#OhBrotherWhereArtThou?

"He Caspered me."

"What's that?"

"It's when you friendly-ghost someone. Like, he stopped initiating dinner plans, but I still see him at yoga every week and we make polite small talk."

Bay Cities. Santa Monica.

#DisappearingAct

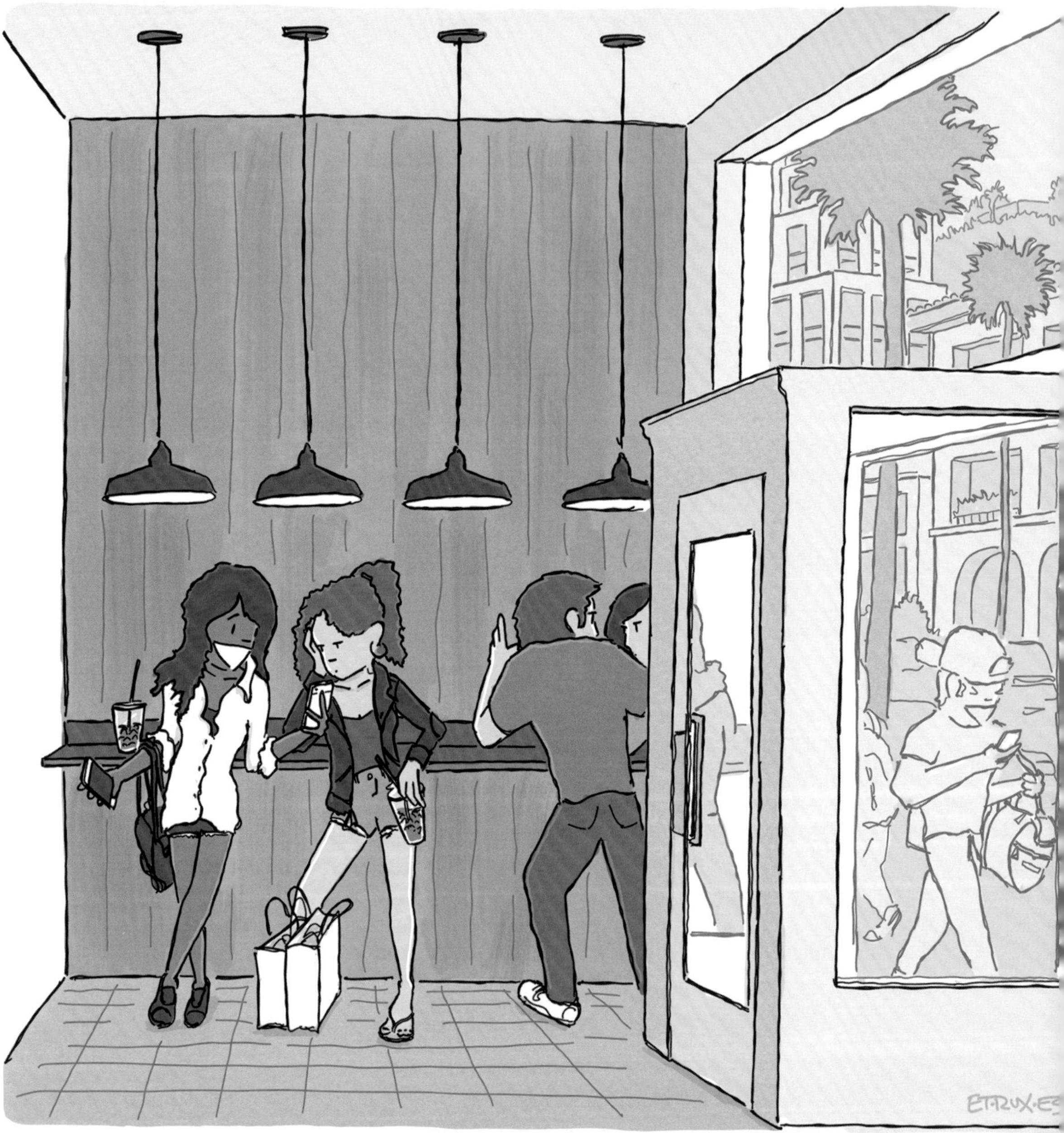

"I'm sorry . . . but his Instagram screams, 'I haven't been faithful once in my entire life.'"

"What are you doing later?"

"I have three dates lined up. A hike with a 6 at 4:00, drinks with a 7 at 7:00, and hopefully those suck because I'm having dinner with a 9 at 8:30."

General Lee's. Chinatown.

#NumbersGame

"We've exchanged a lot of long awkward stares. But I can't ask her out because I'm unemployed right now. I mean I'm selling cars, but I haven't sold one yet."

Erewhon Market. Beverly Blvd.

#DreamJob

"I didn't want to go all the way to SoHo House just to break up with him. That's a pretty upscale place to end things."

Poinsettia Park.

#HighEndEnd

"Ugh, it's so annoying because he lives in Venice and I live in West Hollywood. In L.A. terms, we're in a long-distance relationship."

Cofax. Fairfax.

**May you find someone who will take Lincoln to Palms, cut through Culver City, and make a left on Castle Heights, drive through creepy Beverlywood, make a right on Olympic, and take it to Highland, then cut over to Rossmore through semi-creepy but glamorous Old Hollywood, which turns into Vine, and meet you at your cool new loft (funded by your deceased aunt).

#Distance101

Guy 1: I'm not a hipster.

Guy 2: You send dick pics on Polaroid.

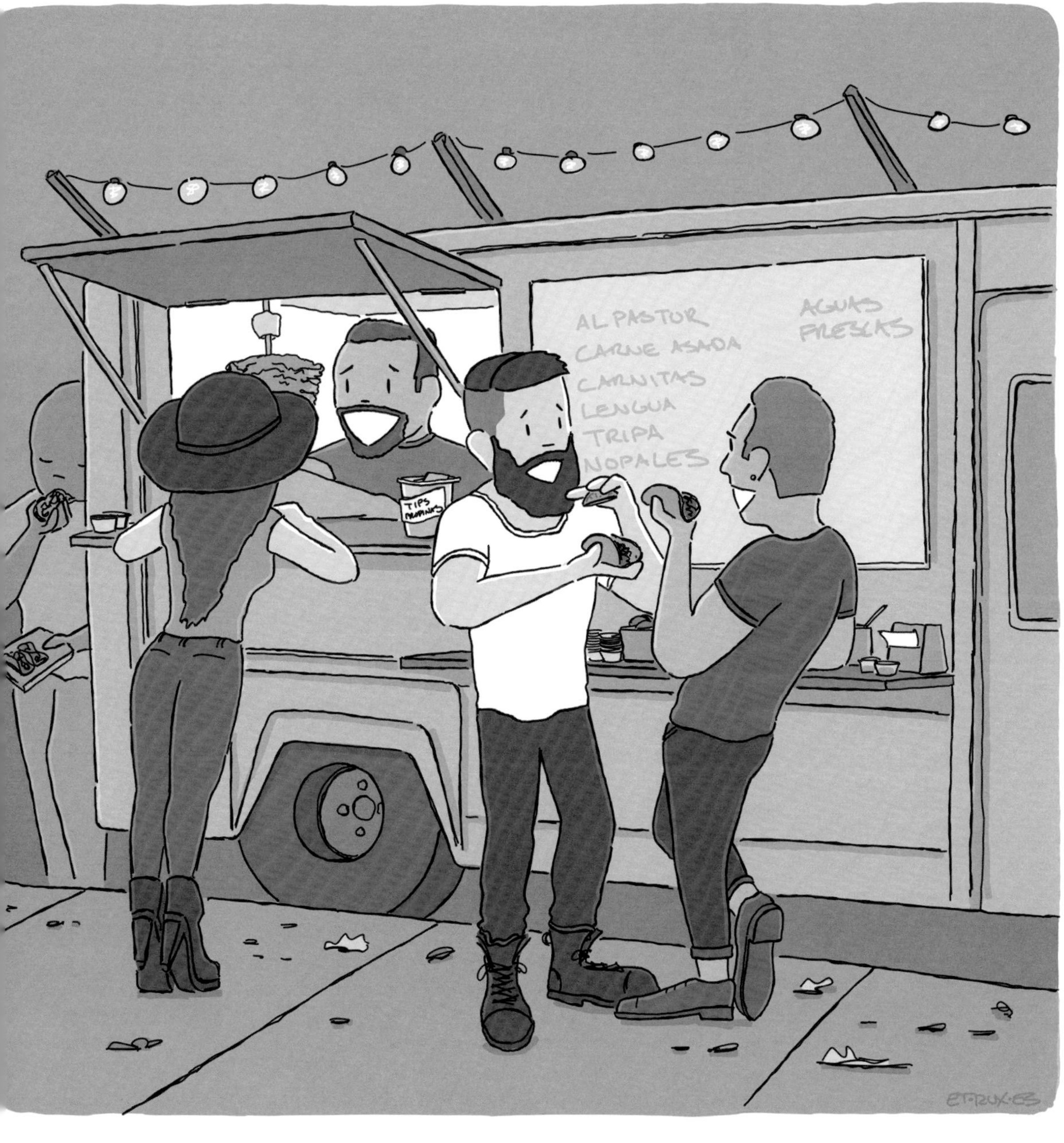
AL PASTOR
CARNE ASADA
CARNITAS
LENGUA
TRIPA
NOPALES
AGUAS FRESCAS
TIPS PROPINAS

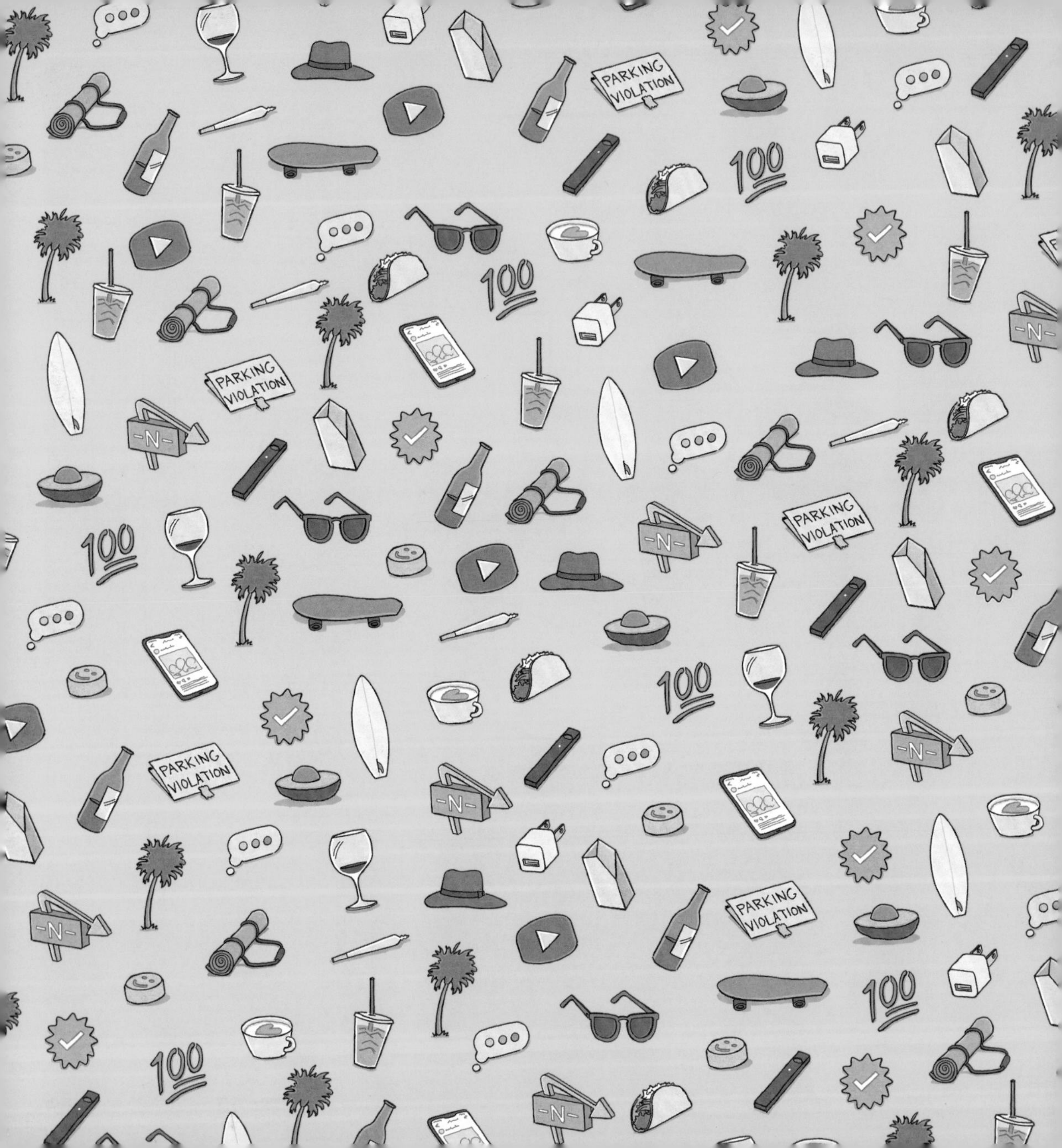
PARKING VIOLATION
100
100
PARKING VIOLATION
-N-
-N-
100
-N-
PARKING VIOLATION
100
PARKING VIOLATION
-N-
-N-
PARKING VIOLATION
-N-
100
100
-N-

#SPIRITUALITY

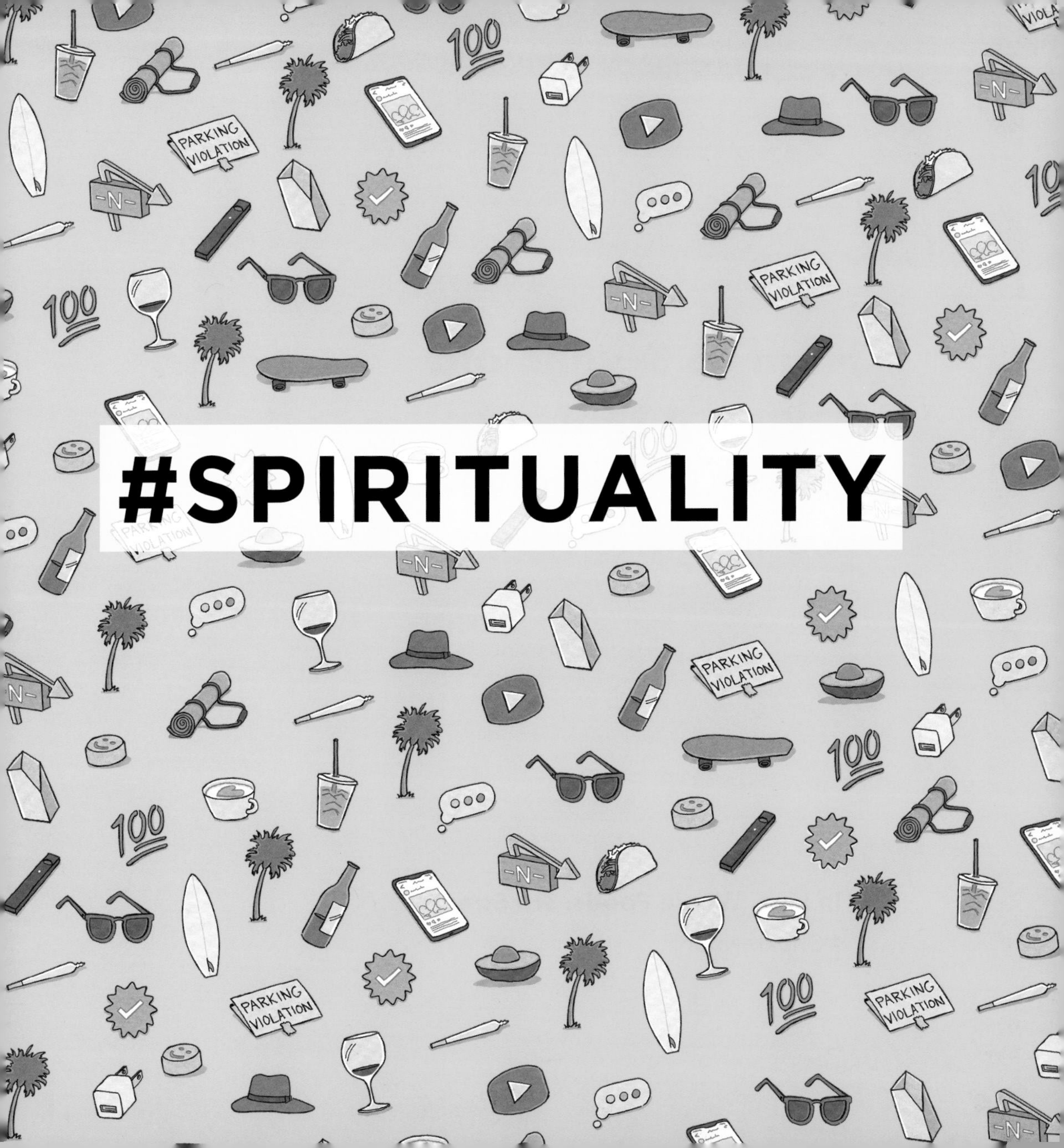
PARKING VIOLATION
100
-N-

Mom to 3-year-old having a tantrum:
"Control your chakras! Control them!"

In Line. Whole Foods. 3rd Street.

#ChakraKhan

"Mercury in retrograde is like the solar system getting its period."

Cafe Gratitude. Venice.

#PlanetaryCycles #SolarHeat

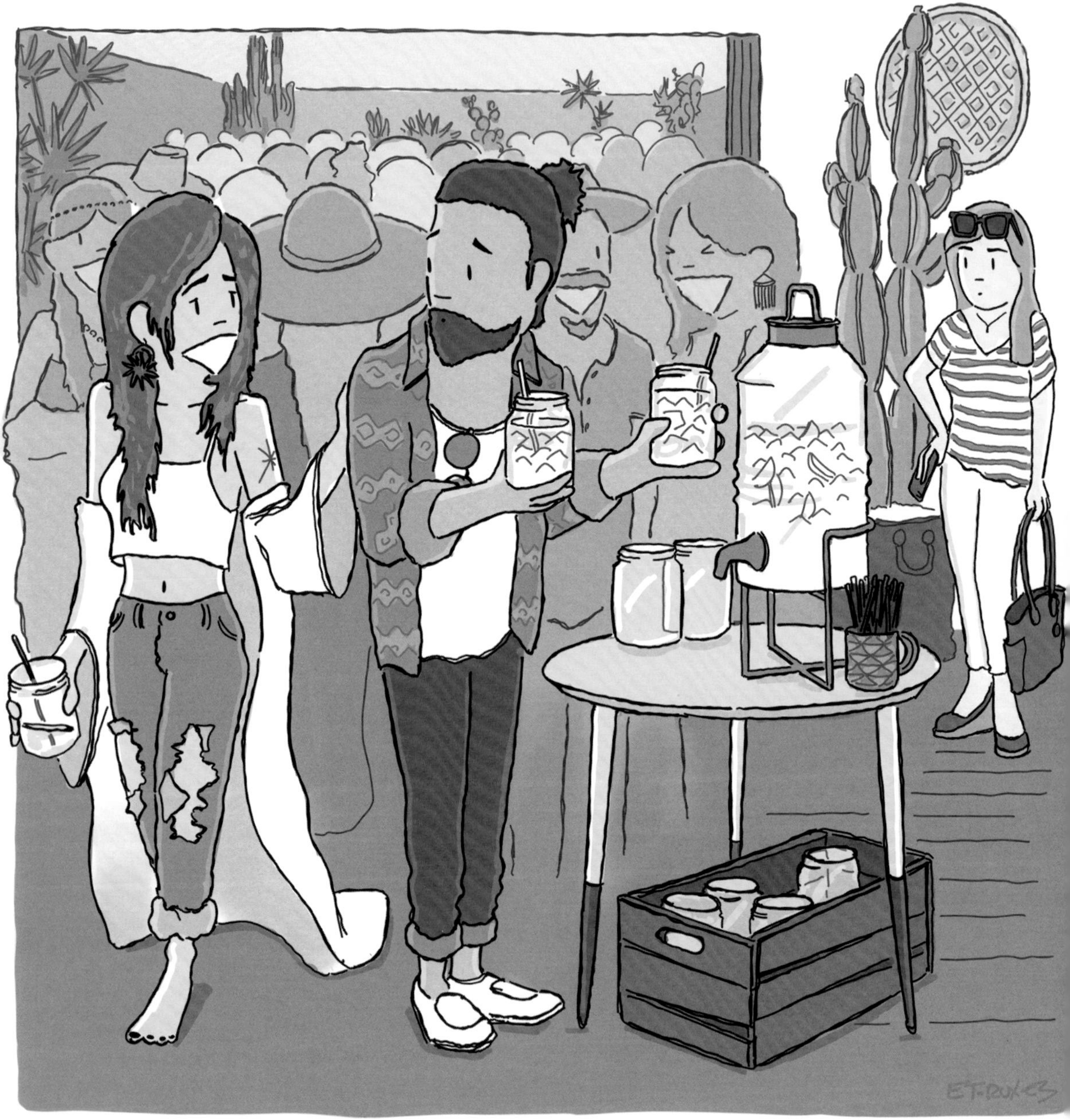

"She's not a bad person but she's just not spiritual . . . like we are."

"He's into something really bad now."

"Drugs?"

"Worse. God."

Party. Mulholland Drive.
**Only in L.A. do people think you're weird if you're Christian, atheist, or just "not that spiritual." But it's totally normal for you to have a traveling healer named Rackoon free your body of dark energy using a combination of illegal frog poison and sage.

#HolyRoller #Rackoon

"After we had sex, he cried and said, 'Namaste.'"

Whole Foods. W. 3rd Street.

#FinalSequence

"Will the customer interested in books on dog reincarnation please come to the information desk?"

Barnes & Noble. Calabasas.

#GoldendoodleSamsara

Judge: State your profession.

Potential juror:
Spiritual advisor. And to clarify,
I already know too much about
this case to serve as an impartial
juror because I'm a clairvoyant.

Santa Monica Courthouse.
#JuryRig

Mother to Son: And what do we say before we leave?

Son to cashier: Namaste.

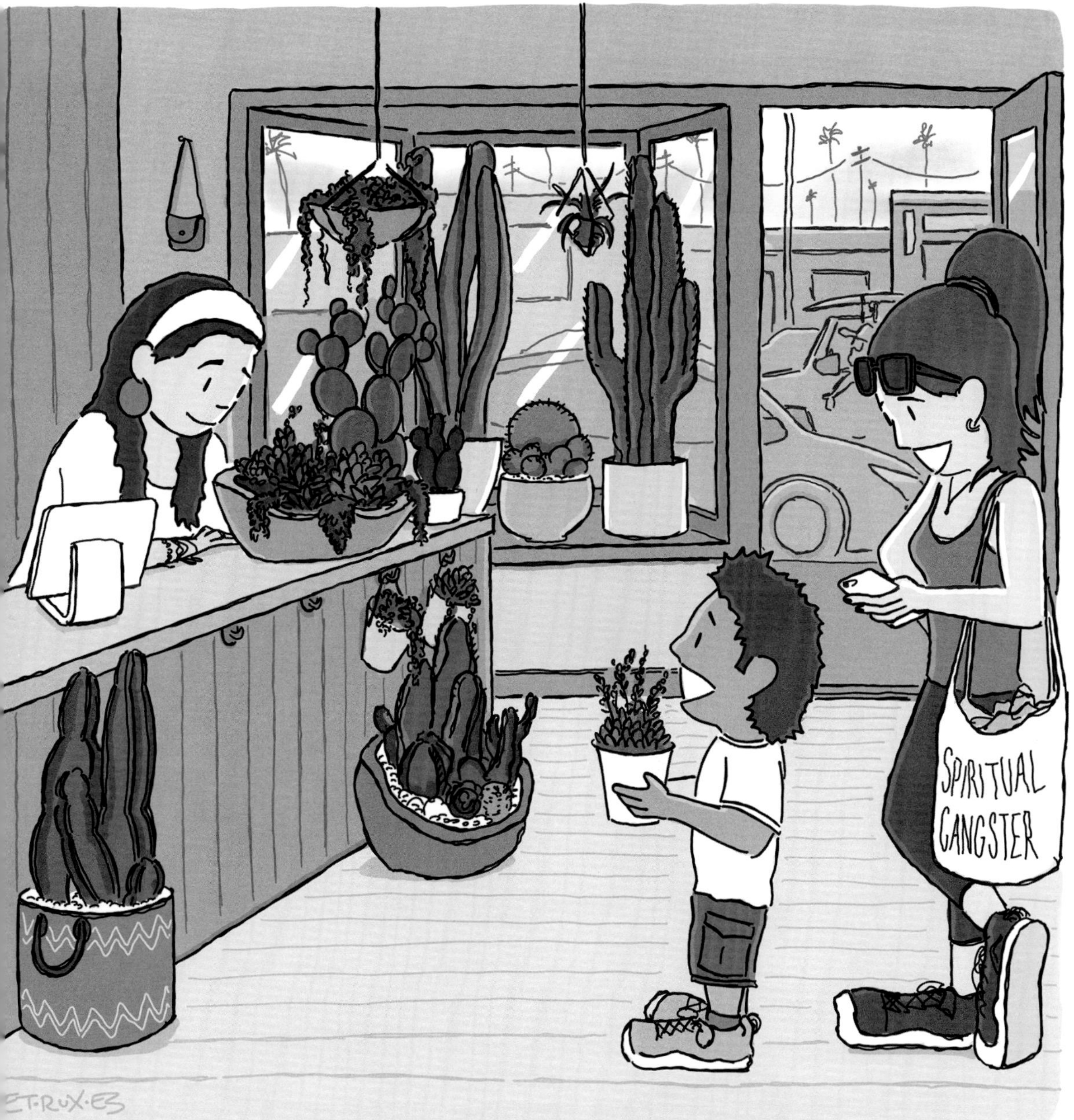

SPIRITUAL
GANGSTER
ET·RUX·EB

"Burning Man wasn't really sexual for me this year. But I did have a three-way make-out session with this hacker dude and a Swedish yoga gnome."

French Market Cafe. Venice.

#Zoolander3:PlayaEdition #gnomaste

"I think she's going through something."

"Why?"

"She started meditating and hiking. Nobody does that when they're happy."

Pasadena City College.

#SelfHelp

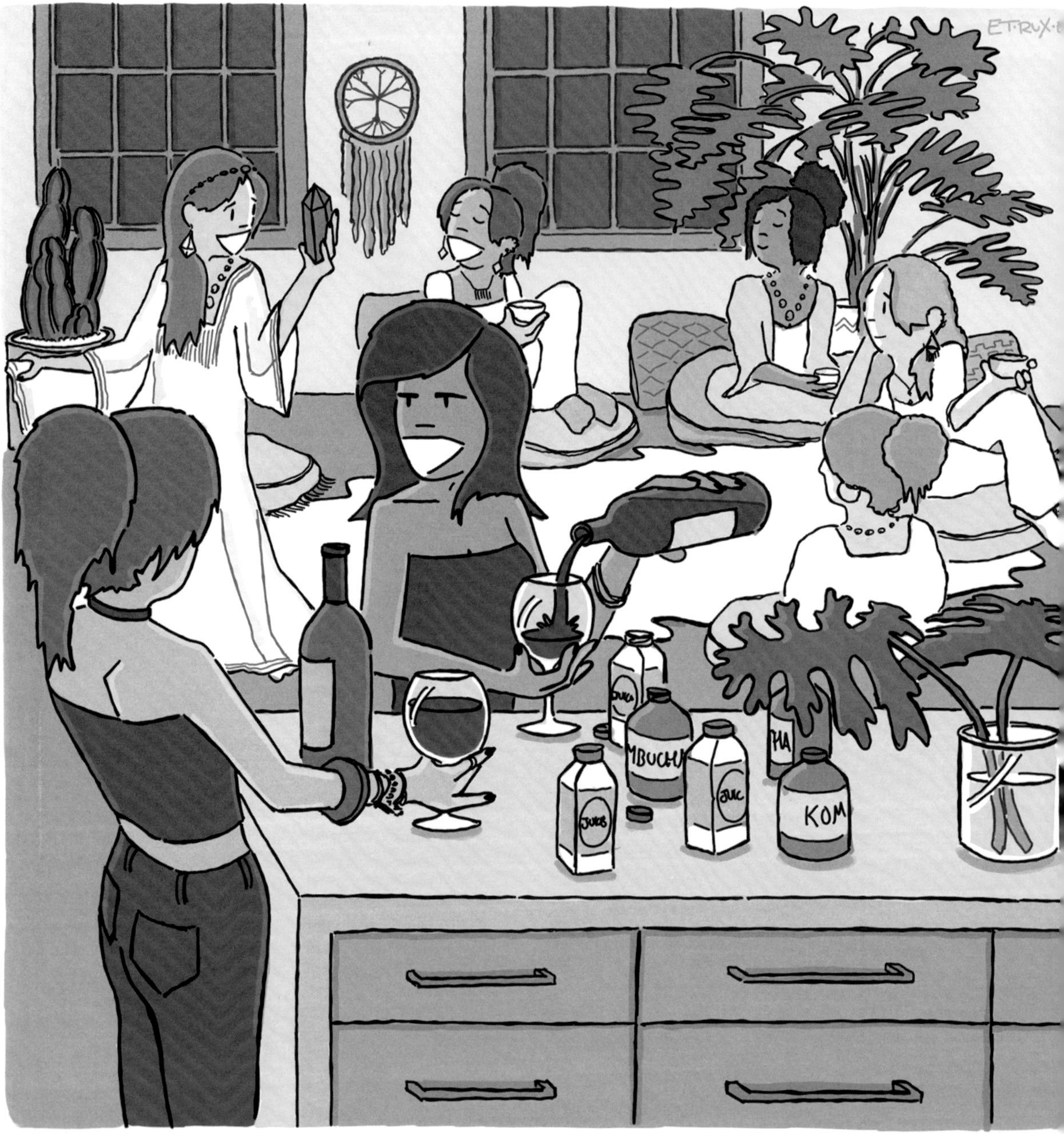
MBUCHA
KOM

Girl 1: She went away for a few days and came back enlightened.

Girl 2: Where did she go?

Girl 1: Coachella.

"You went to Burning Man,
not Iraq, calm down."

Pasadena.

#MilitaryOutfit

Police officer to friend:
"I pulled a lady over who was on her phone while driving. She said, 'Thanks. I've been needing an intervention like this for some time.'"

Cabo Cantina. Santa Monica.

#intervention

"Spirituality has become fashion. Forget about actually working on yourself; just spend $400 on crystals and hang a bunch of air plants on your bedroom wall and you're 'enlightened.'"

Hinano Cafe.

#AestheticAscetic

"He's really sensitive right now;
he just got back from Oakland."

"Fuck, did something happen?"

"Ayahuasca."

Here's Looking at You. Koreatown.

#GuidedTour

Lady: Your son is adorable, how old is he?

Mother: Oh no, we don't do age . . . We're infinite beings walking this Earth.

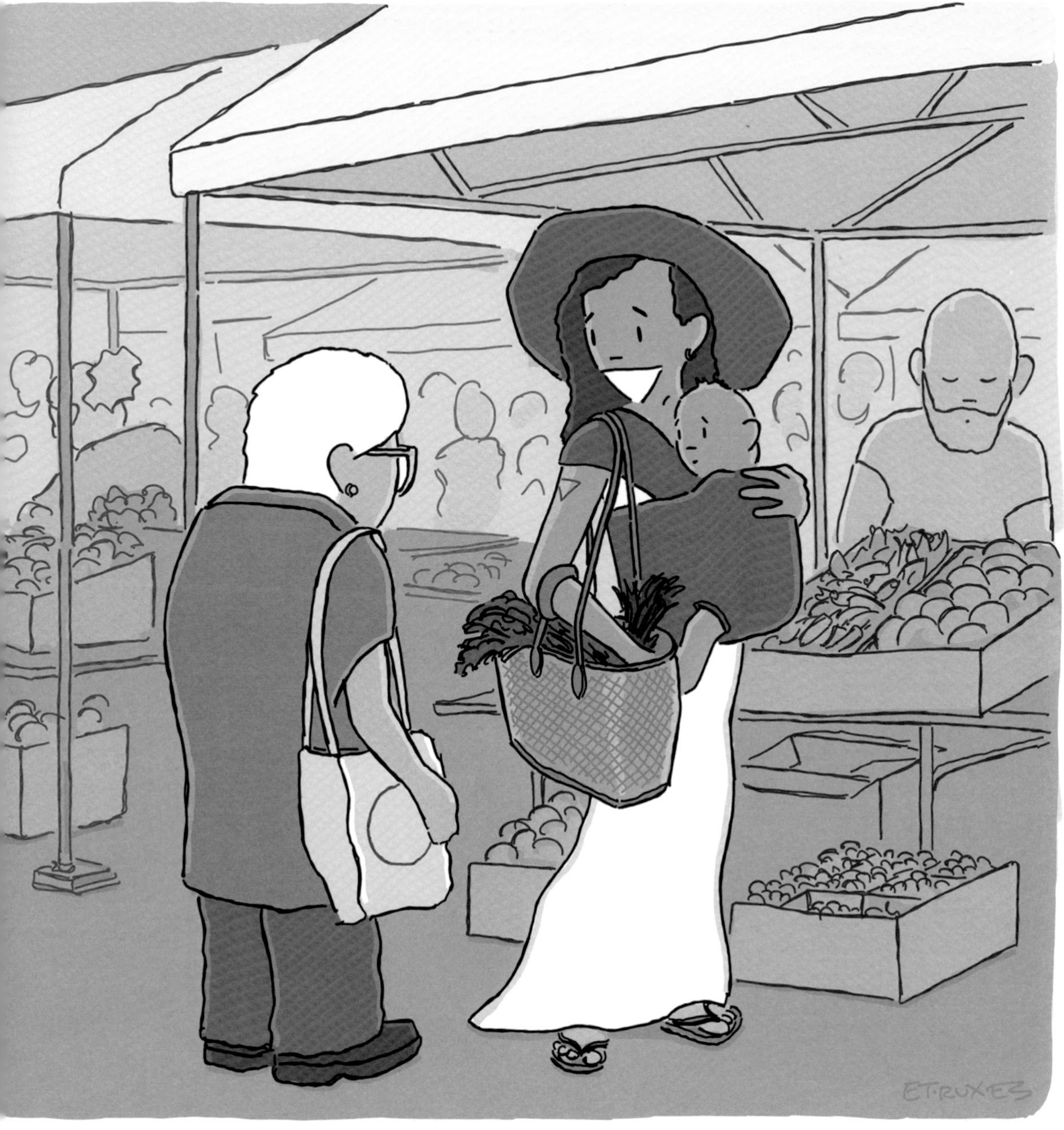

"They should do a remake of *Aladdin* where the genie comes out of a Himalayan salt lamp."

Party. Hancock Park.

#ILoveLamp

"We drove to Joshua Tree to trip but forgot our mushroom chocolates at home. The cleaning lady ate the whole bar and has been tripping for three days."

Couple. Topanga.

#Fungicide

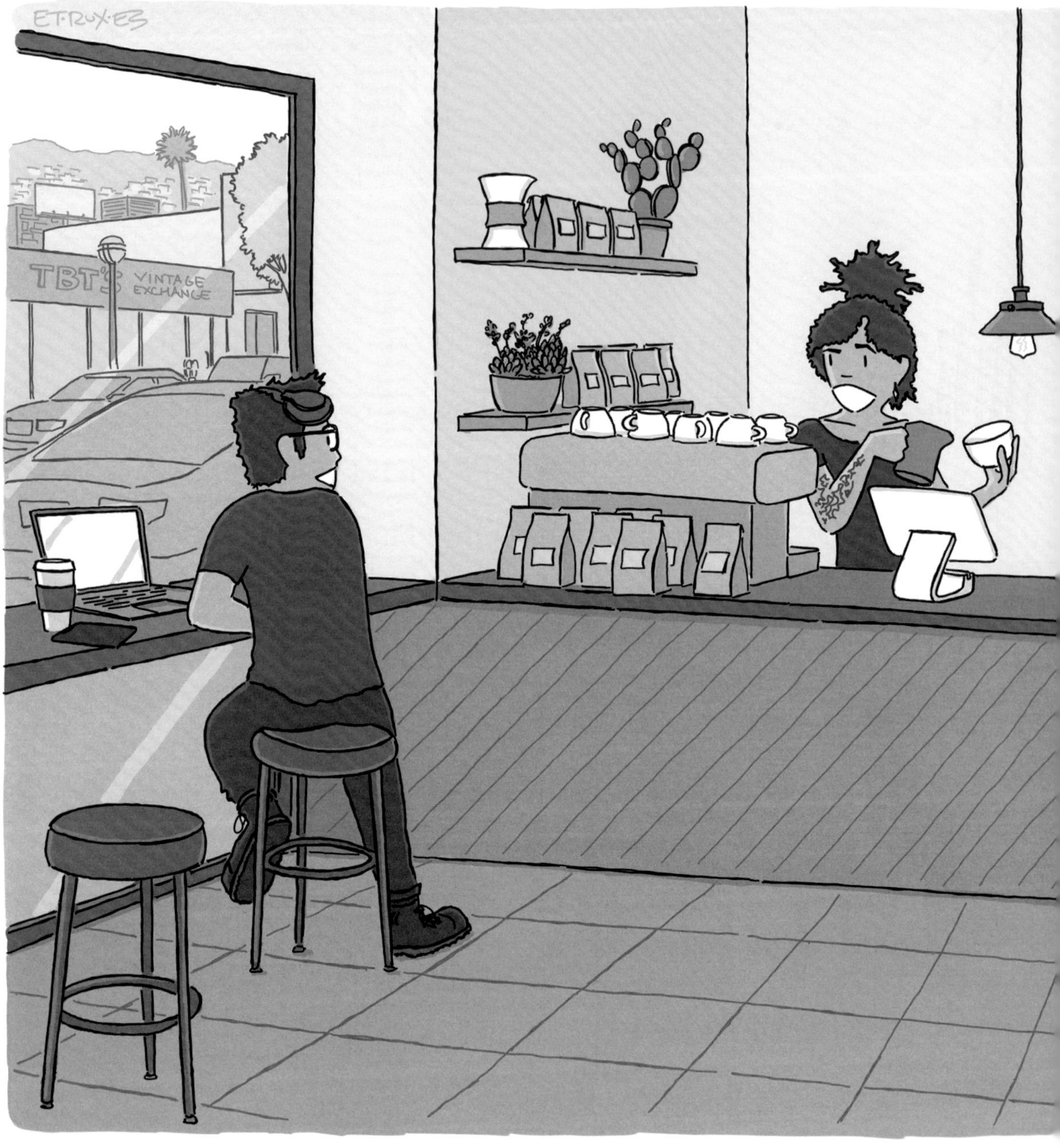
TBT'S VINTAGE EXCHANGE

Customer: You close at 6:30, right?

Barista: Yeah, but we close emotionally at 6:00.

"I've got this ugly bump on my eye. My crystal healer thinks it's definitely a blocked tear duct."

"What does your doctor say?"

"I don't have one."

Blue Bottle. Venice.

#HealingCircle

Owner talking about her dog:

"Crouton got a tarot reading. She had a past life in Elizabethan times and was choked by her lover. That's why she doesn't like being picked up. The psychic could also tell she was a Pisces."

Atmosphere Cafe.

#CanineReincarnation

"I live alone in a forest of likes."

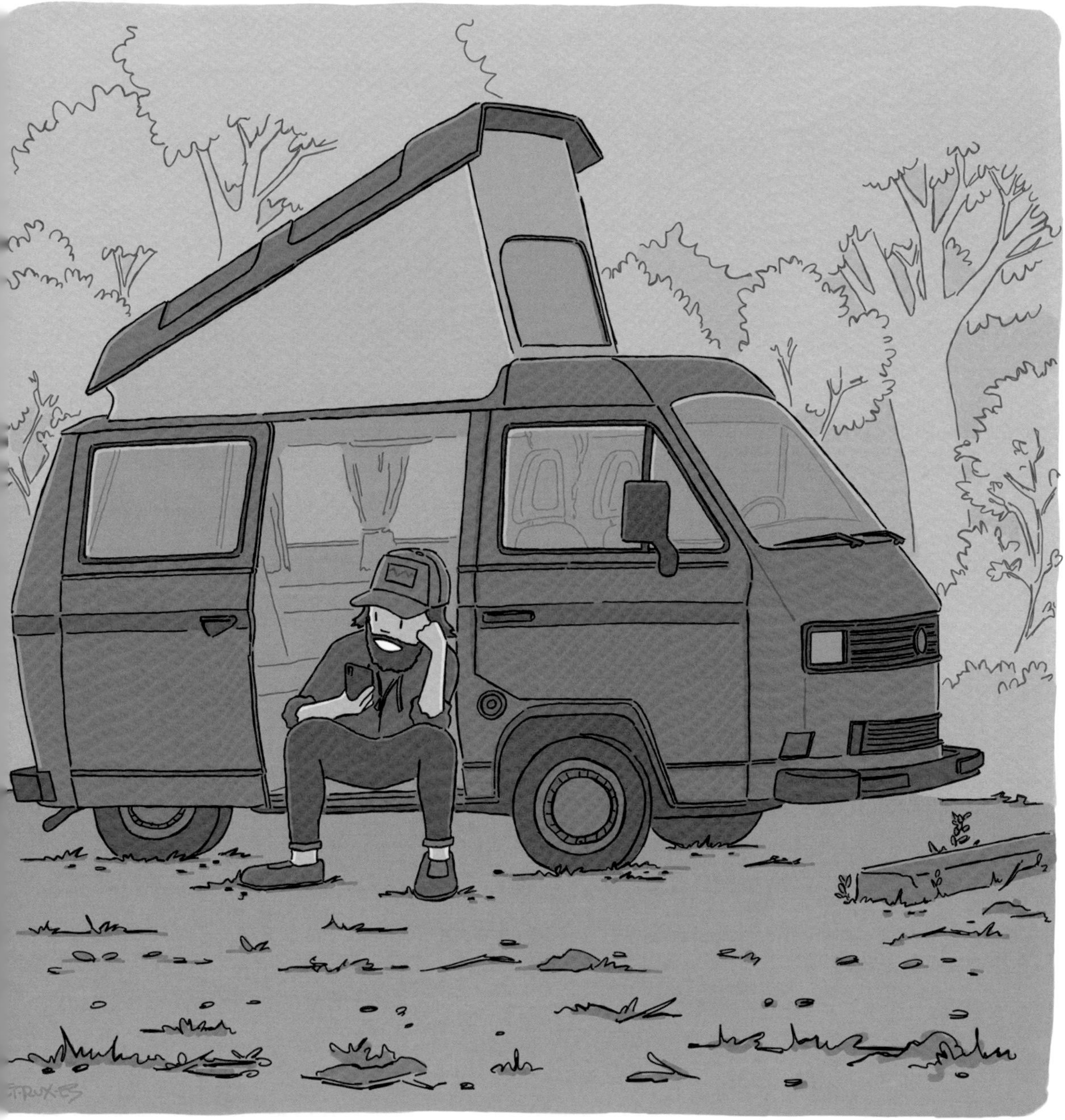

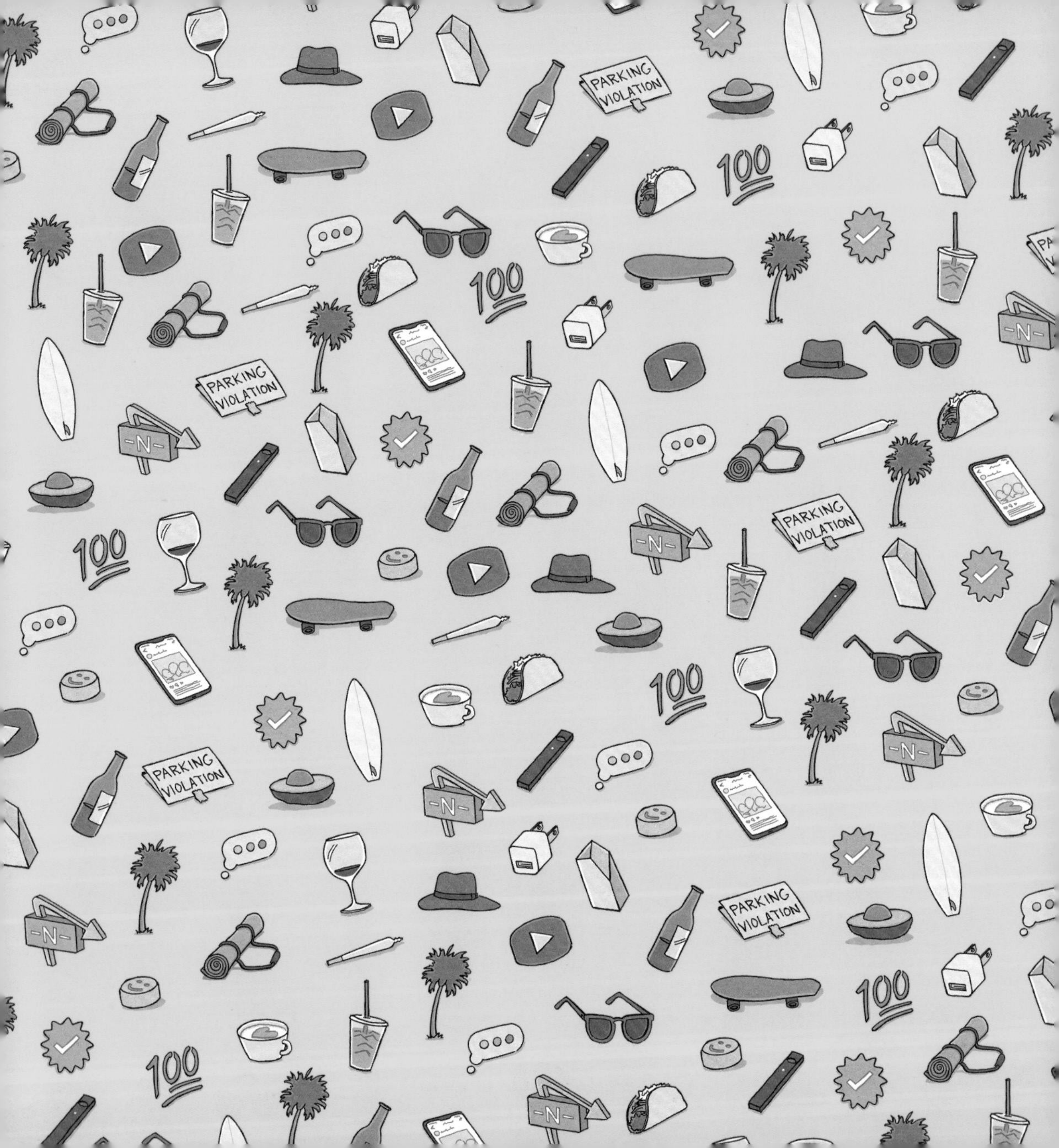
PARKING VIOLATION
100
-N-

#FOOD

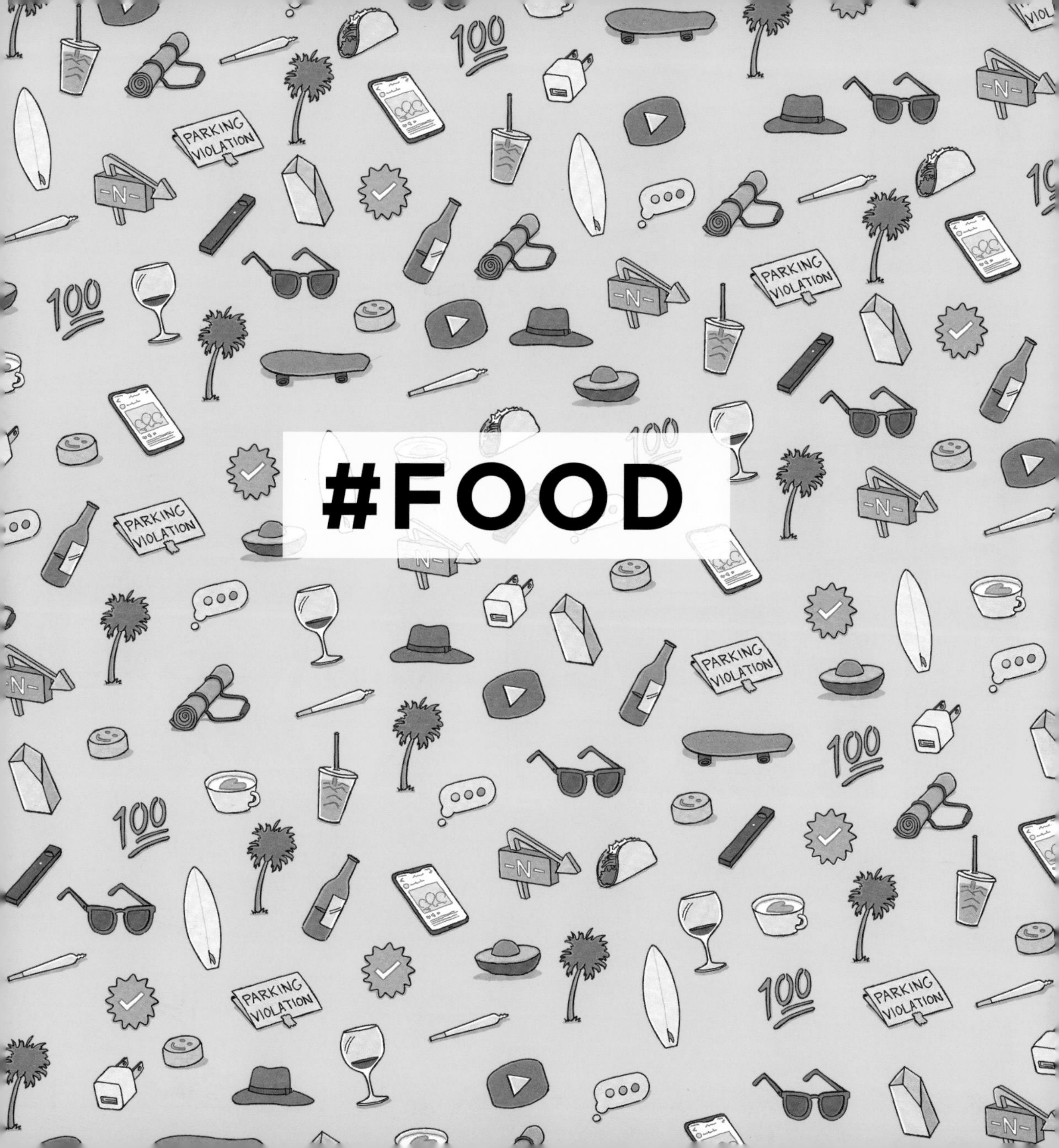
PARKING VIOLATION
100
-N-

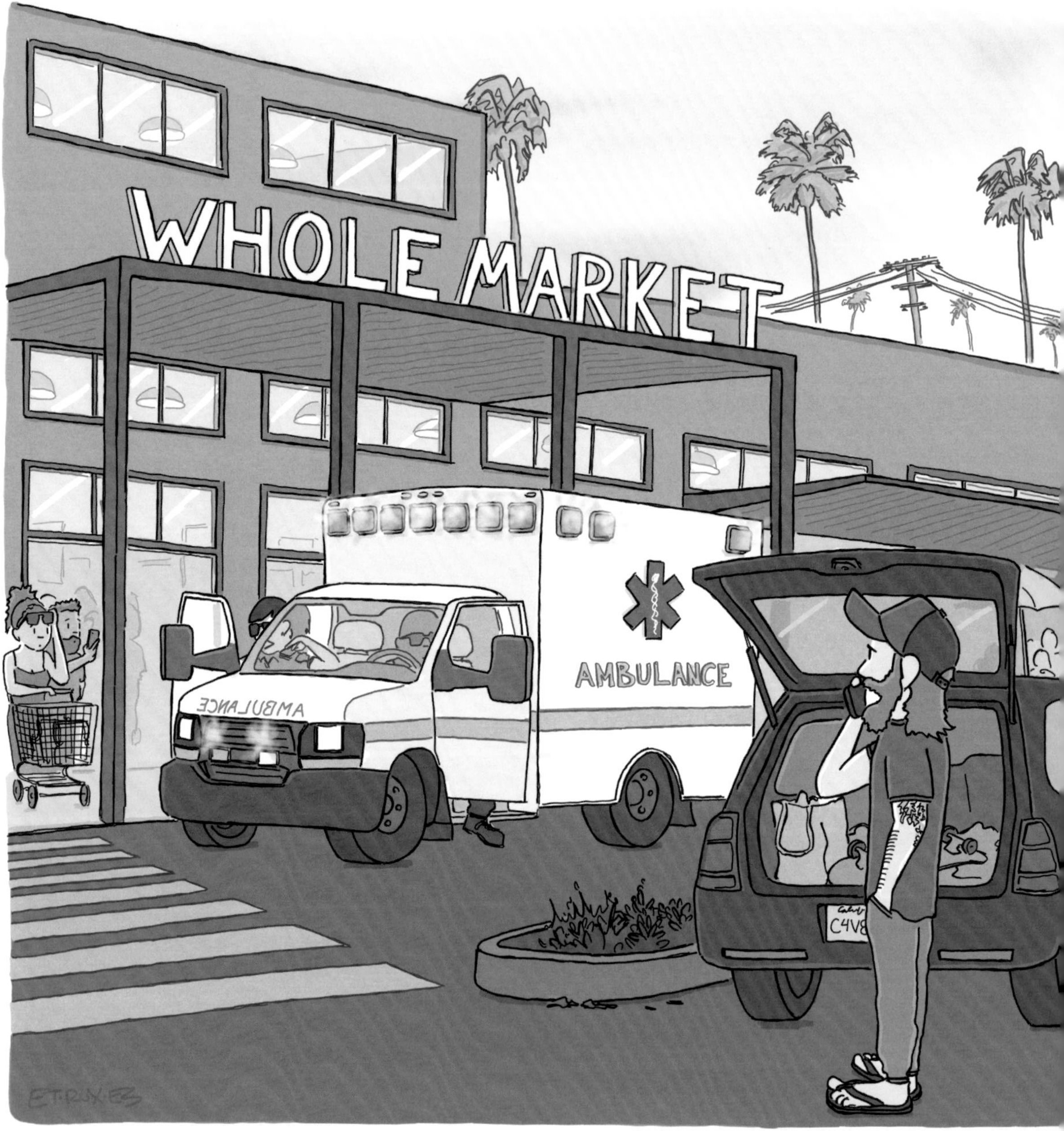
WHOLE MARKET
AMBULANCE
AMBULANCE
C4V8
E.T.ROUX.E3

"Somebody must have accidentally eaten gluten."

"She goes to college in Iowa."

"Oh my God. Why does she go there?"

"I have literally no idea, but her mom sends her weekly shipments of avocados."

UCLA Sorority House.

#HealthyFats

"I can't afford anything I'm doing. Like a matcha latte is literally 45 minutes of work."

Pressed. Brentwood.

**Stop wasting your money on $7 lavender lattes with "persimmon mylk" and do cool shit … visit Bhutan, trip out with polyamorous shamans and WME agents at Burning Man, or buy a house in Atwater Village in March of 2020.

#MatchaTime

Soho House employee: I'm sorry, sir, we don't allow outside beverages.

Guy: You're not TSA. Don't do this to me. I just spent $8 on this coffee.

Soho House. West Hollywood.
#HipsterTSA

"You can't be vegan in jail."

In line. LAX.

#ProteinBars

"Hi! I would like to place an order to go. Yeah, can I get that thing you just posted on Instagram?"

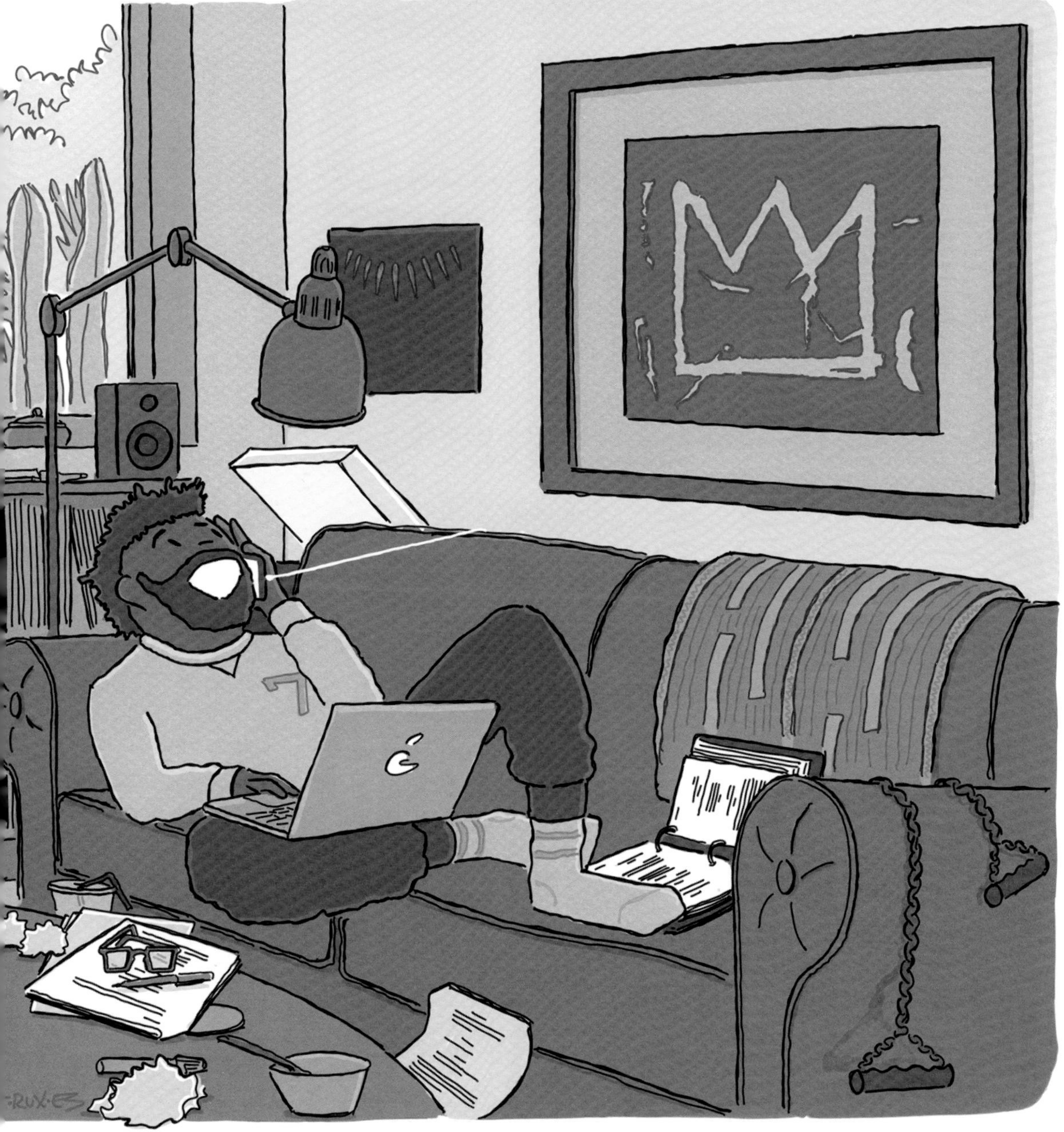

"I'm down to three avocados a day."

Little Pine.
#GreenParty

"The Elixir is a single-origin coffee brewed with sound waves. Today's selection was brewed to Prince's *Purple Rain*."

Copa Vida. Pasadena.

#WhatDoesYourCoffeeListenTo #DJbarista

"If I'd never bought bottled water, I'd be a homeowner."

Trader Joe's. Toluca Lake.

**You haven't left town in six months, but you've had water from 16 different countries.

#LiquidAssets

"You really love iced coffee. I've been with you six years, and you've never looked at me the way you looked at the barista when they called your name."

Blue Bottle Coffee. Arts District.

#BeverageInfidelity

"I'll have a soy White Mocha."

"Oh, you're lactose intolerant?"

"No, I'm just complicated."

Starbucks. Studio City.

#labyrinthine

Cashier: How are you today?

Customer: Okay.

Cashier: Life isn't supposed to be lived "just okay."

Customer: Look, I just came here for some coconut water. Not a fucking life coach.

Trader Joe's. West Hollywood.
#RetailTherapy

Lady: Hi, do you have soy milk?

Barista: We have almond, coconut, and oat.

Lady: Why no soy?

Random customer: It's not 2003.

Alfred. Melrose Place.
#nutsHell

"I can't stand the peaches at Whole Foods. They don't respect the peach community. I can see the mold from over 6,000 feet away. Have you seen *American Sniper*? That's me spotting mold."

Hollywood Farmers' Market.

#OrganicSniper

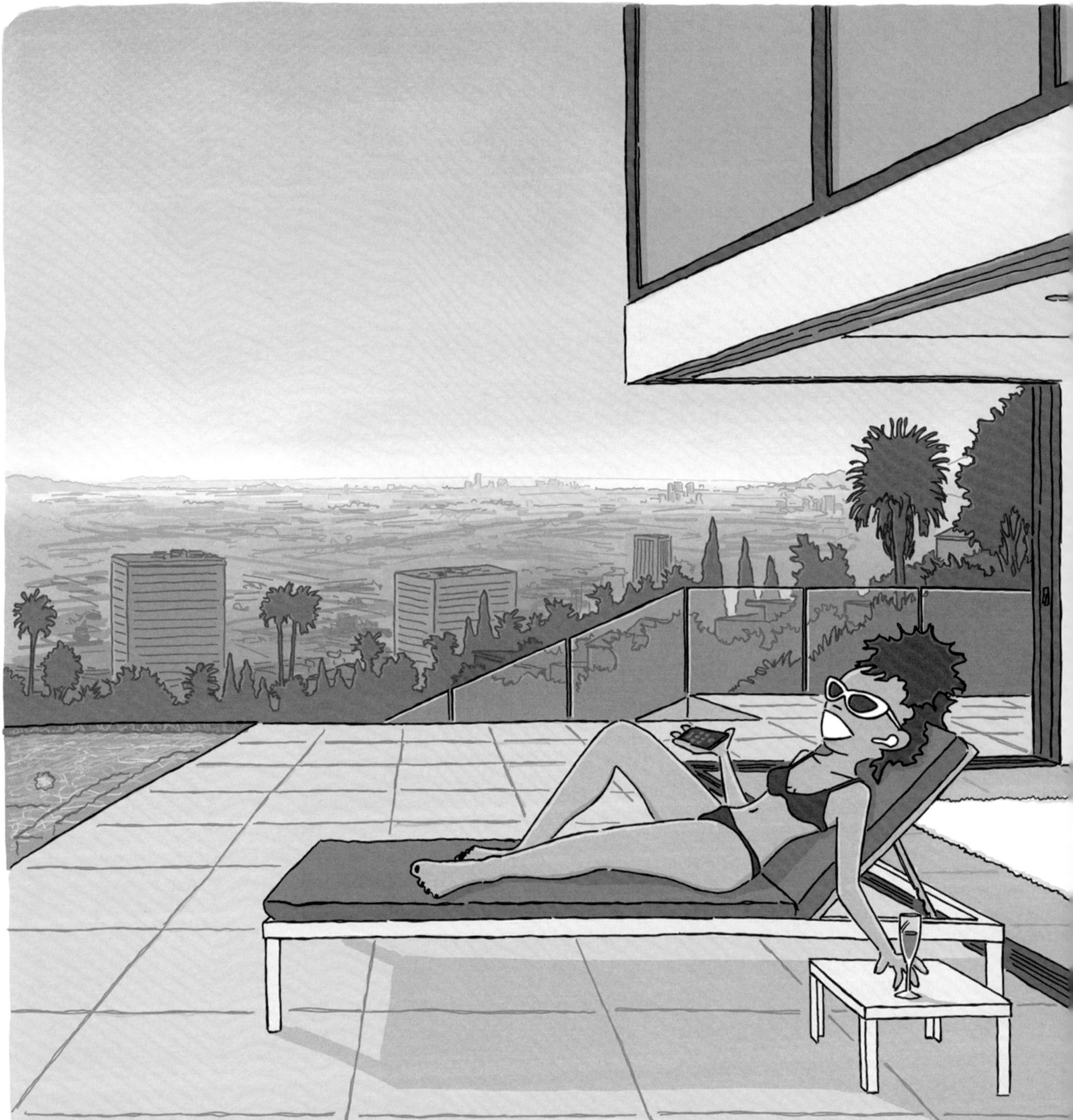
ET·RUX·ES

"I completely blacked out, but apparently was able to log my 3 a.m. burrito into my calorie counter."

"That Uber Eats guy was so sweet. He's from a random country, like one you only hear about during the Olympics."

Dinner Party. Newport Beach.

#TheAmericans

"How many Blue Apron meals do I need to cook for assholes before I find my husband?"

Father's Office.

#BlueIsTheLamestColor

"Kale is the basic bitch of leafy greens. Kale got lucky, made a sex tape, and is now a popular, useless vegetable."

Dinner party. Echo Park.

#KaleKardashian

Three women:

"Okay. Fuck, marry, kill: Trader Joe's, Whole Foods, Sprouts. GO!"

Revolution Speakeasy. Agoura Hills.

#SupermarketFantasy

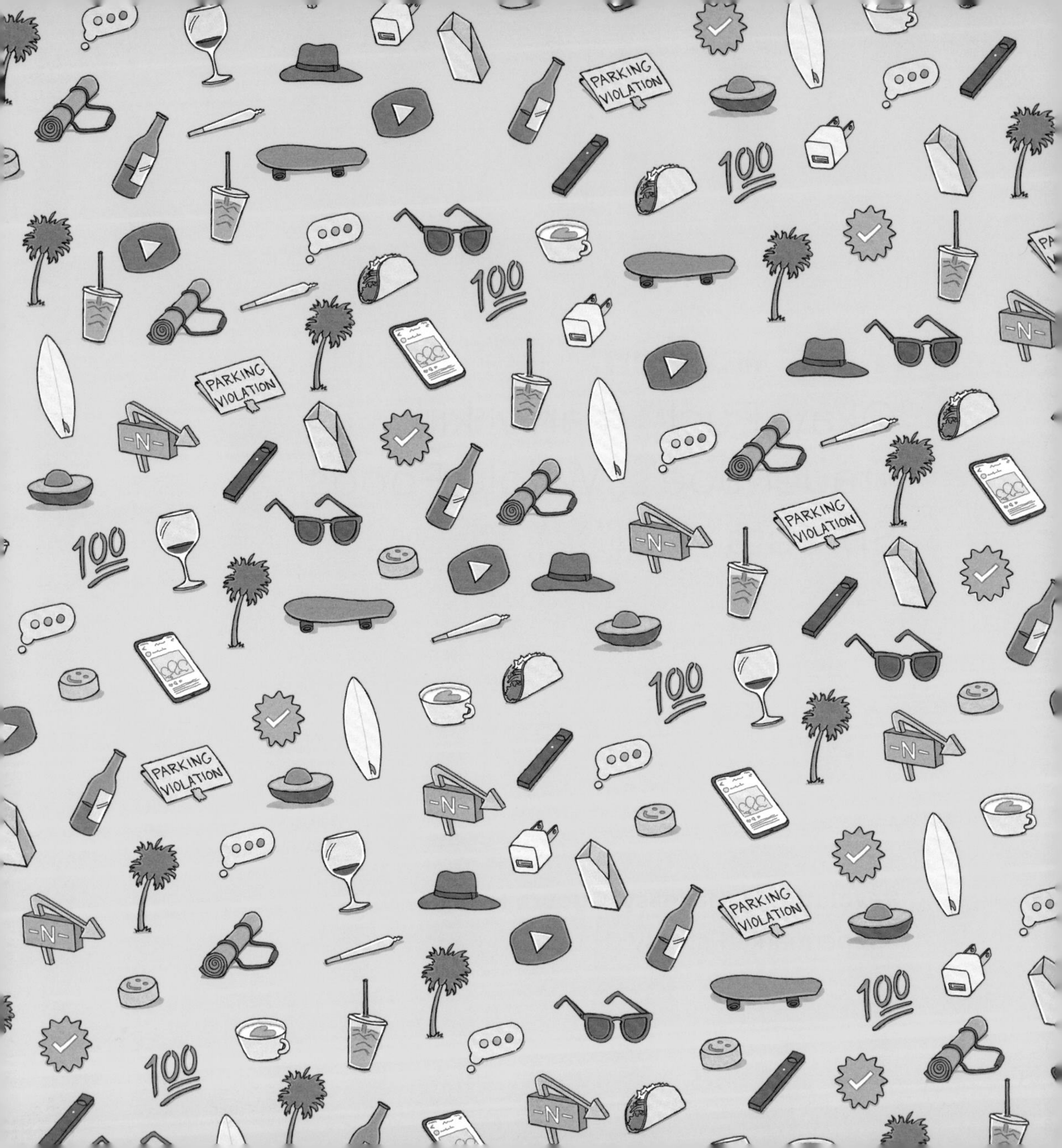
PARKING VIOLATION
100
100
-N-
PARKING VIOLATION
-N-
PARKING VIOLATION
100
-N-
100
PARKING VIOLATION
-N-
-N-
-N-
PARKING VIOLATION
100
100
-N-

#HEALTH AND FITNESS

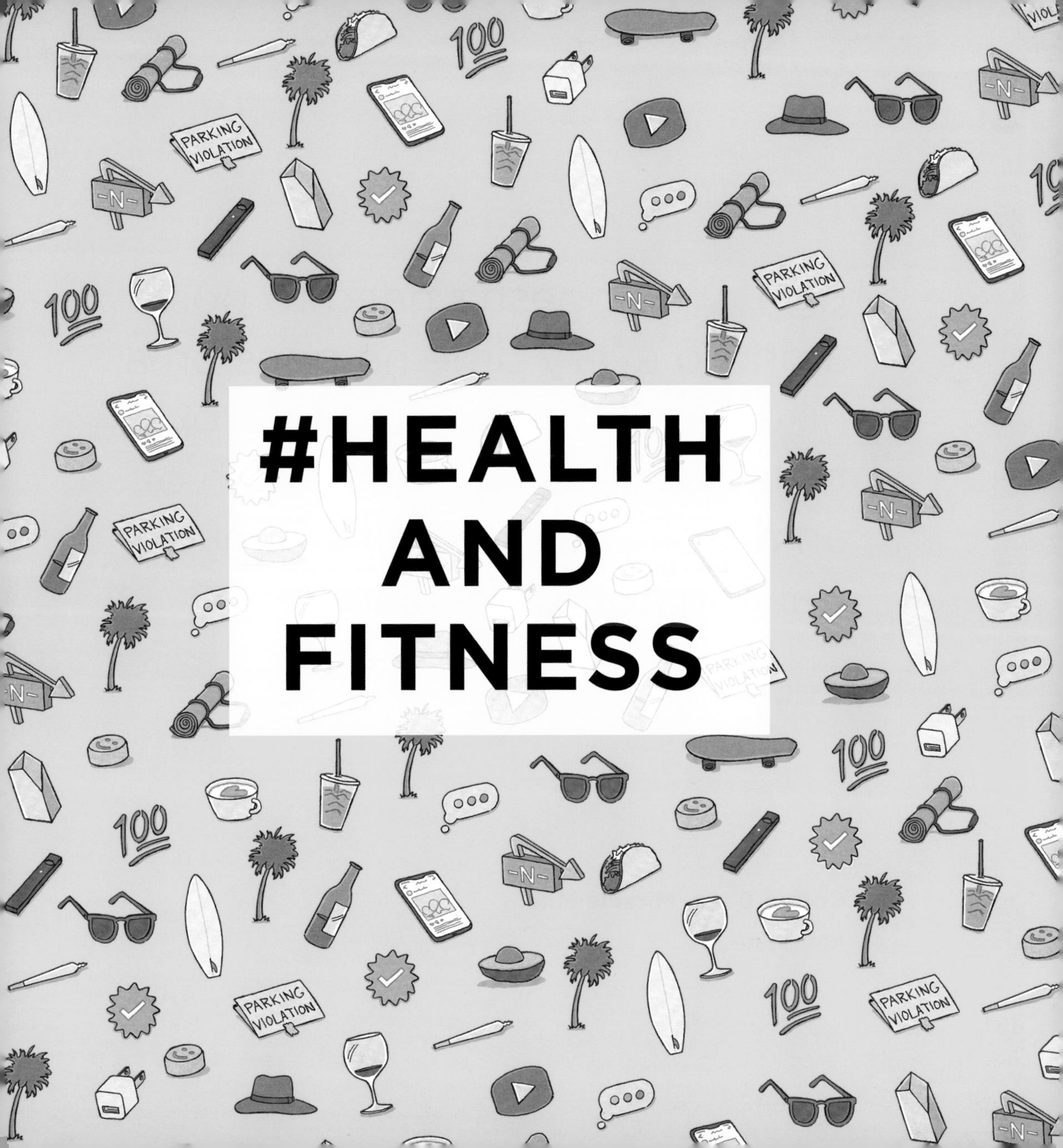
PARKING VIOLATION
100
-N-

"Ugh . . . he doesn't need to post a photo every time he goes on a hike. Don't get me wrong, I love hiking. It's just not that much of an accomplishment. It's Runyon Canyon not Kilimanjaro."

Coffee Bean. Miracle Mile.

#MtSelfie

"I started listening to angry rap music at the gym today. You can't deadlift to 'This American Life,' you know what I mean?"

L.A. Fitness. Culver City.

#NPReps

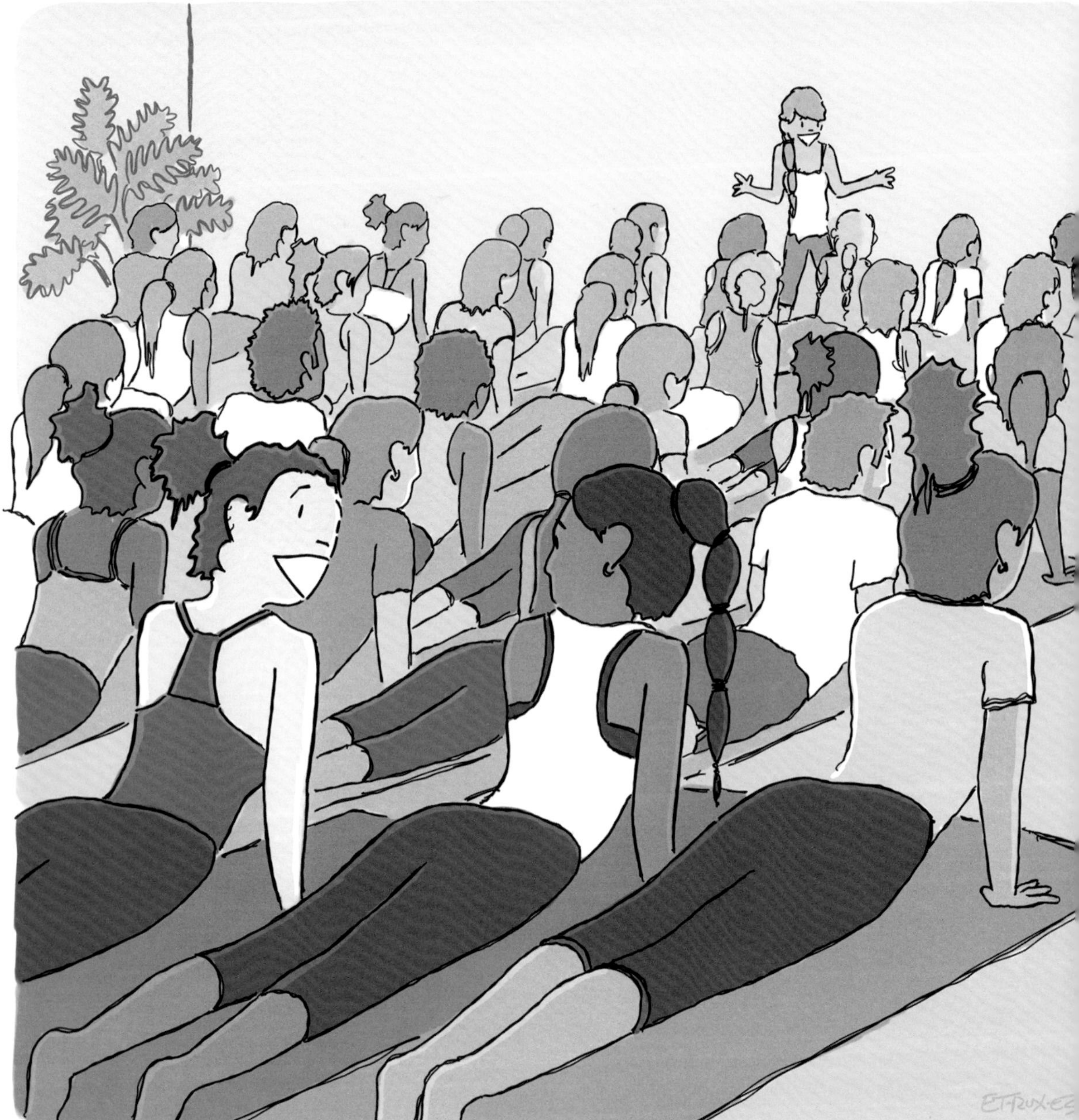

"I love yoga. But I hate that people think it automatically makes you spiritual. There are a lot of flexible psychos in this city."

"How do you get your ass so toned?"

"I do squats holding my Maltese."

Starbucks. Westwood.

#DogTrainer

"Your body says 'Westside,' but your soul says 'Eastside.'"

Millie's. Silver Lake.

#BestOfBothWorlds

"I've started this new workout called urban hiking."

"Isn't that just walking?"

Iroha Sushi of Tokyo. Studio City.

#Peripathetic

Yoga teacher:

"Whoever is breathing like they are doing lines of coke right now: STOP. And yeah, I've done it plenty so I know what it sounds like, okay?"

Equinox. Beverly Hills.

#AlternateNostrilBreathing

In line to register for yoga class:
"Excuse me . . . Can you hurry the fuck up?? There are other people waiting."

Wanderlust Yoga Studio.

#DickPose

"I wish I liked jogging.
It's like free exercise ..."

LAMILL. Silver Lake.

#FreeRunning

Runner to dog:
"Don't be a cliché.
You're better than that."

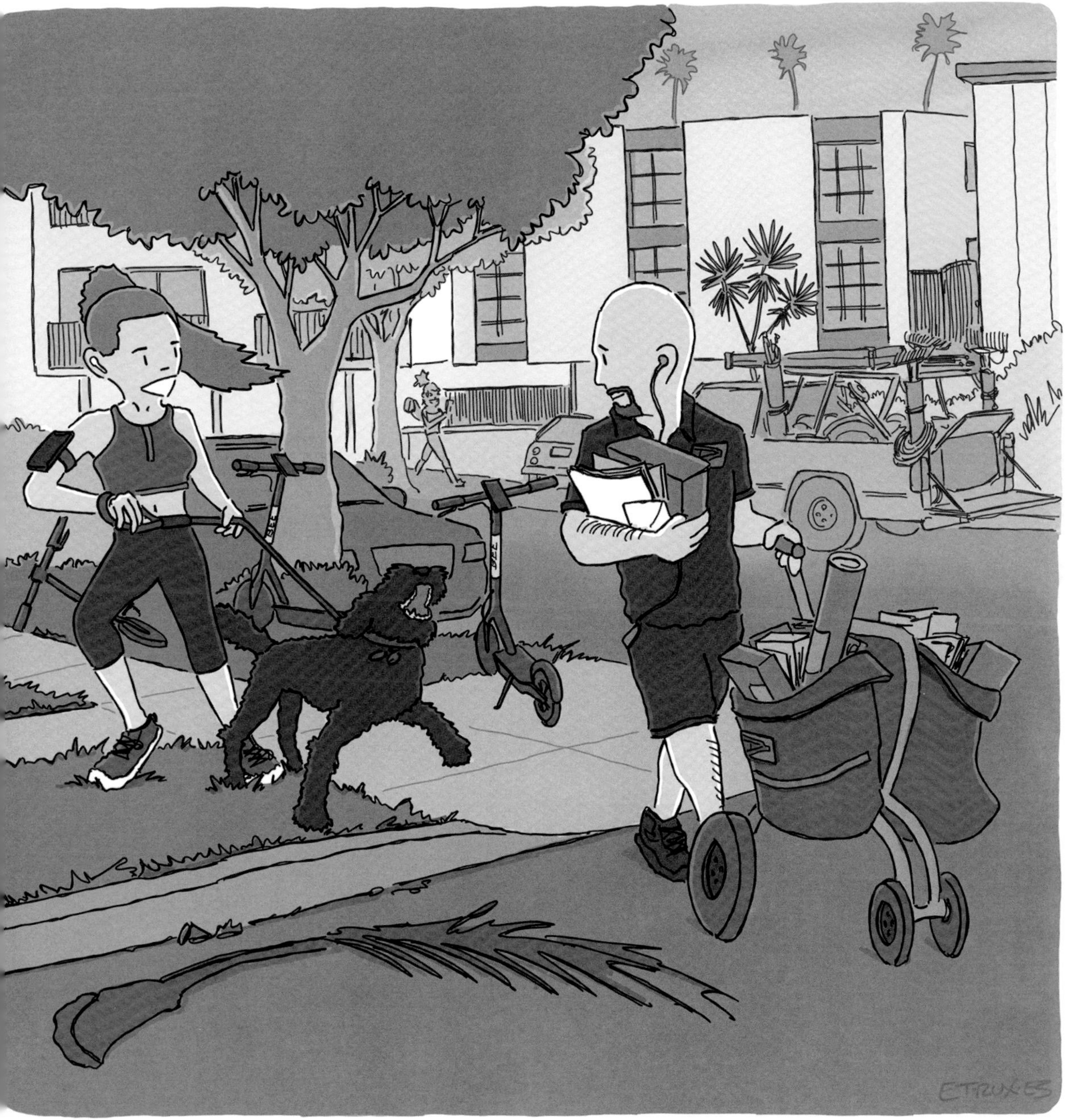
ETRUXES

Yoga instructor to class:

"Now we're going to do chair pose. Pretend like you don't want to sit on that Porta Potty seat at Coachella. And exhale."

Yoga Studio. Mar Vista.

#BasicYoga

Lawyer: What gear were you in at the moment of impact?

Witness: Lululemon leggings and Nikes.

Lawyer and Witness. L.A. Superior Court.

#NoJudgment

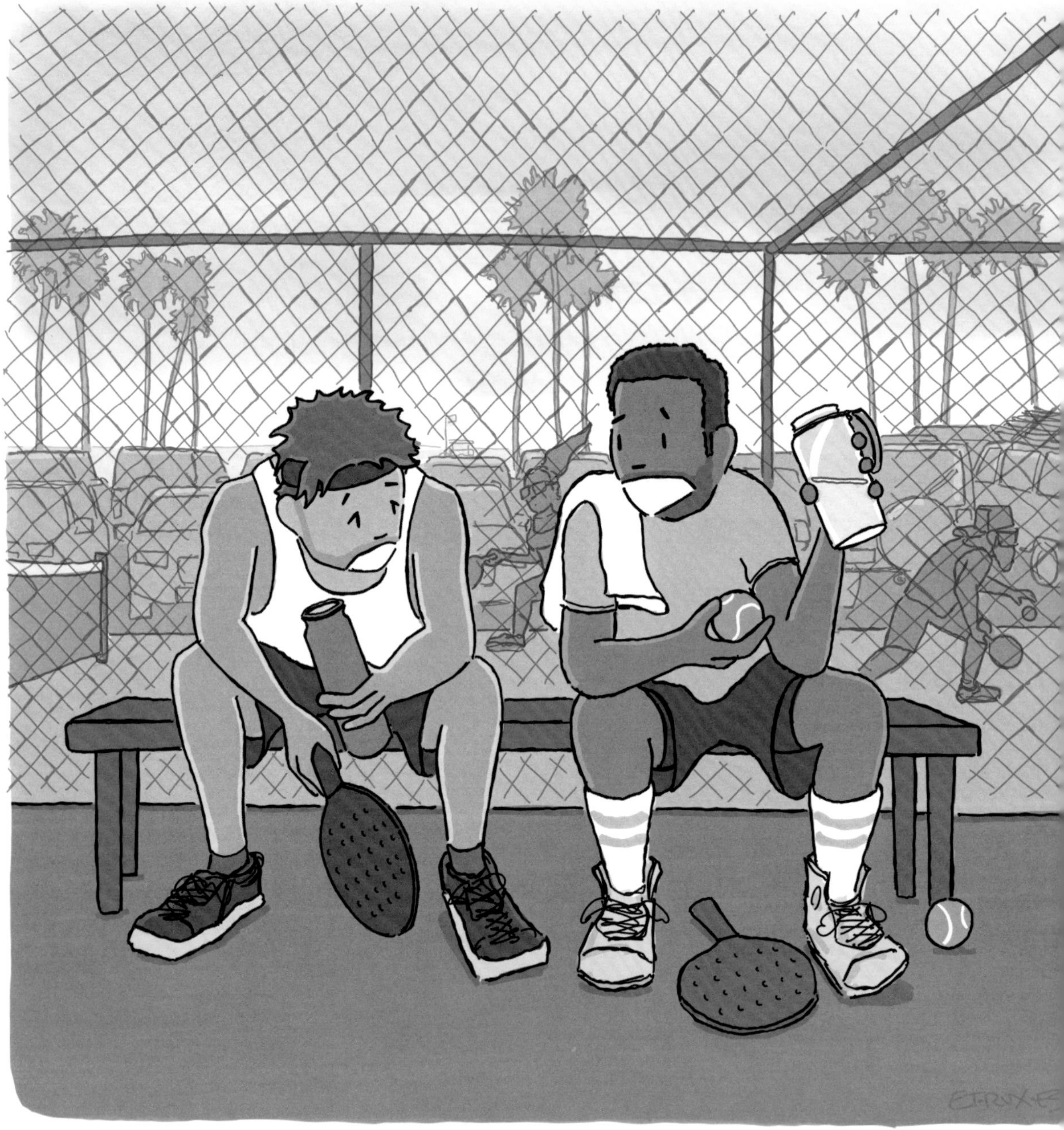

Guy 1: She's perfect, dude. Cute. Smart. Thinks I'm funny. Doesn't care that I'm not rich.

Guy 2: So what's the problem?

Guy 1: She's a Clippers fan.

"I'm going to be a hot yoga instructor now."

"Good luck. You're maybe a 4."

"Hot yoga is a type of yoga, you idiot."

Law Office. Orange County.
#HotOrNot

"Oh, I love this corset waist trainer. Where's it from? I've been meaning to get one."

"Um . . . this is my scoliosis brace."

Granville. Studio City.

#FashionMistake

"We randomly fill up each other's Hydro Flasks. It's our love language."

Sugarfish. Studio City.

#TheShapeOfWater

Fitness instructor: "Guys, these planks are more stable than any relationship I've ever had."

Workout Class. Studio City.

#StableGenius

"So then I said to him, 'I don't care how many big waves you've surfed, bro. You're a pompous guy with no spiritual merit.'"

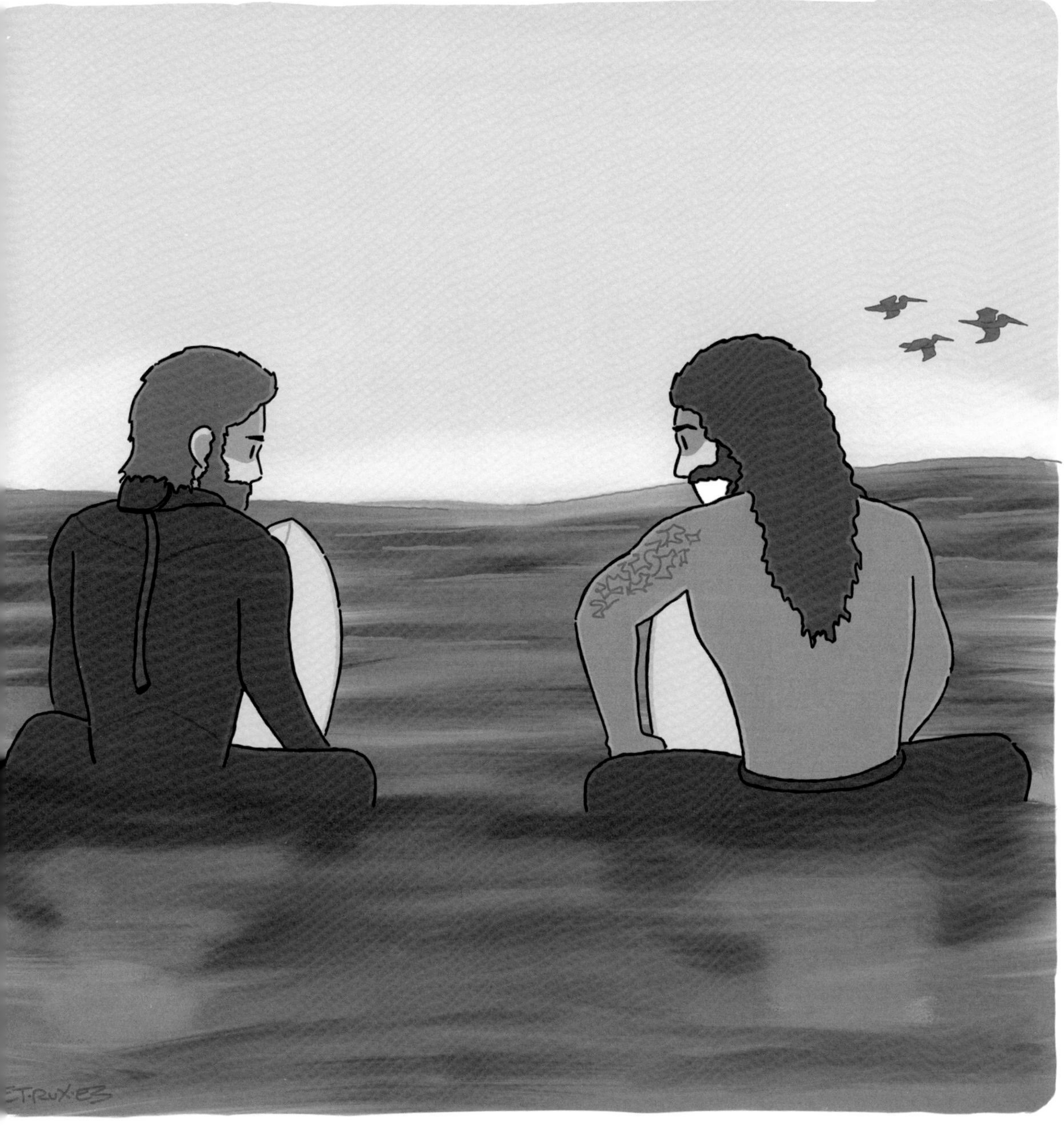

SoulCycle instructor to class:
"Jen is not only killing the arm series, but she is also literally creating human life within her. What's your excuse?"

SoulCycle. Beverly Hills.
#BirthCycle

"Dude, you used to sip gin and juice. Now you sip *ginger* juice. What the hell happened to you?"

Wilshire Blvd.

#Downgraded

Valet: Which one is your key?

Girl: It's the one with a CorePower yoga tag. Black tag means unlimited yoga.

Valet: I don't know if that'll help me . . .

Herringbone. Santa Monica.

#limitless

"Do you surf?"

"Nah, I just dress like I do."

Party. Venice.

#CostumeParty

"Babe, please do not ask the guy that works at the juice bar for health advice. He's a part-time employee with a rainbow headband, not a fucking doctor."

Sunset Junction.

#DoctorWho

"Everyone here is physically healthy and emotionally unstable."

Santa Monica Pier.

#WorkoutFreaks

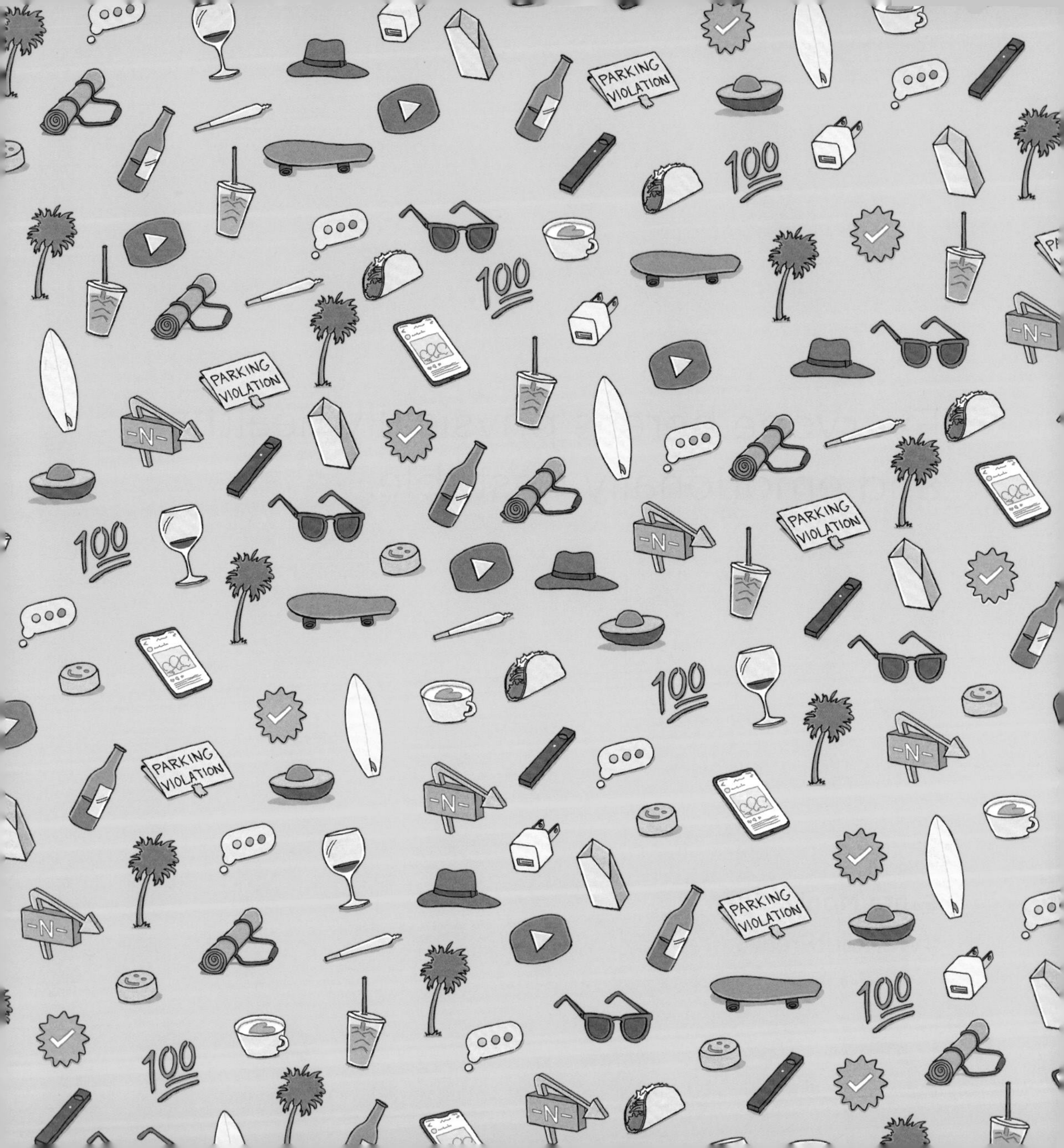
PARKING VIOLATION
100
-N-

#THEYOUTHS
(AND A FEW DOGS)

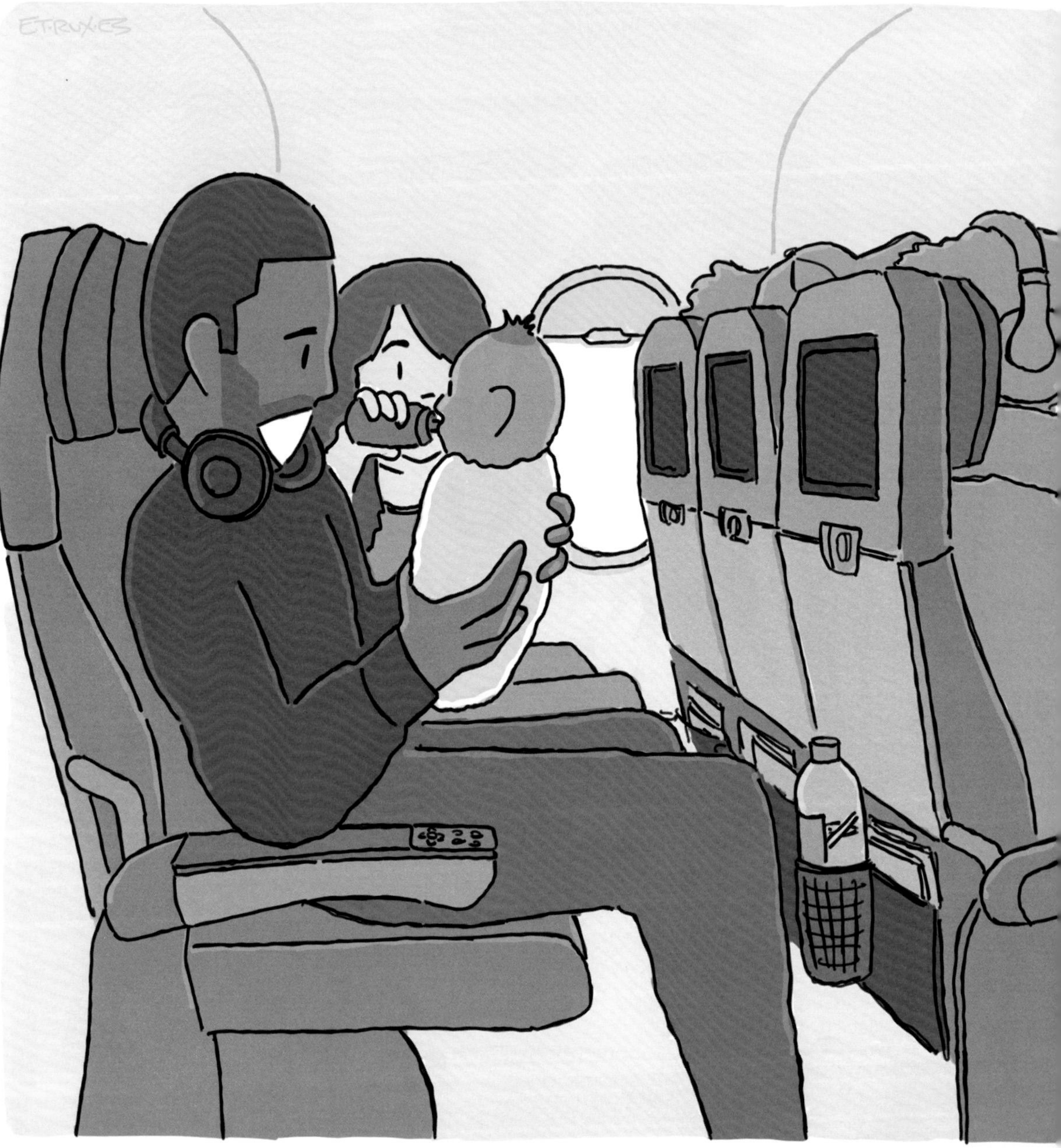

"Be a good baby, okay? Don't fuck this up for everyone."

4th grade girls:

"You look like a hipster."

"What's a hipster?"

"A person that has long hair and is lonely but doesn't know why."

Elementary School. Alhambra.

#FedorasCoverTheLonelyHair

Kindergarten teacher:
Hi, class. Now that summer is over, who can tell me about the four seasons?

Boy: I can! My favorite one is in Maui.

School.
#HotelSchool

Mom to adult son: "We're going to put one cookie on each plate. The one that says 'basic bitch' is for your sister, Emma."

South Pasadena.

#CookieMonster

Babysitter: What did you dream about last night?

7-year-old: I don't dream. I only have nightmares about this economy.

Progressive Parents Meeting. Santa Monica.

#PiggyBankProblems

Two 10-year-olds hugging a tree outside Whole Foods:

Girl 1: Hashtag best friends!

Girl 2: Hashtag vegan!

Westwood.
#GameOfTag

Mom: How was school today?

Daughter: Good.

Mom: What did you do?

Daughter: Just pay attention to the road and don't worry about it.

Venice.
#RoadWarrior

"Get down from there! We don't have health insurance right now!"

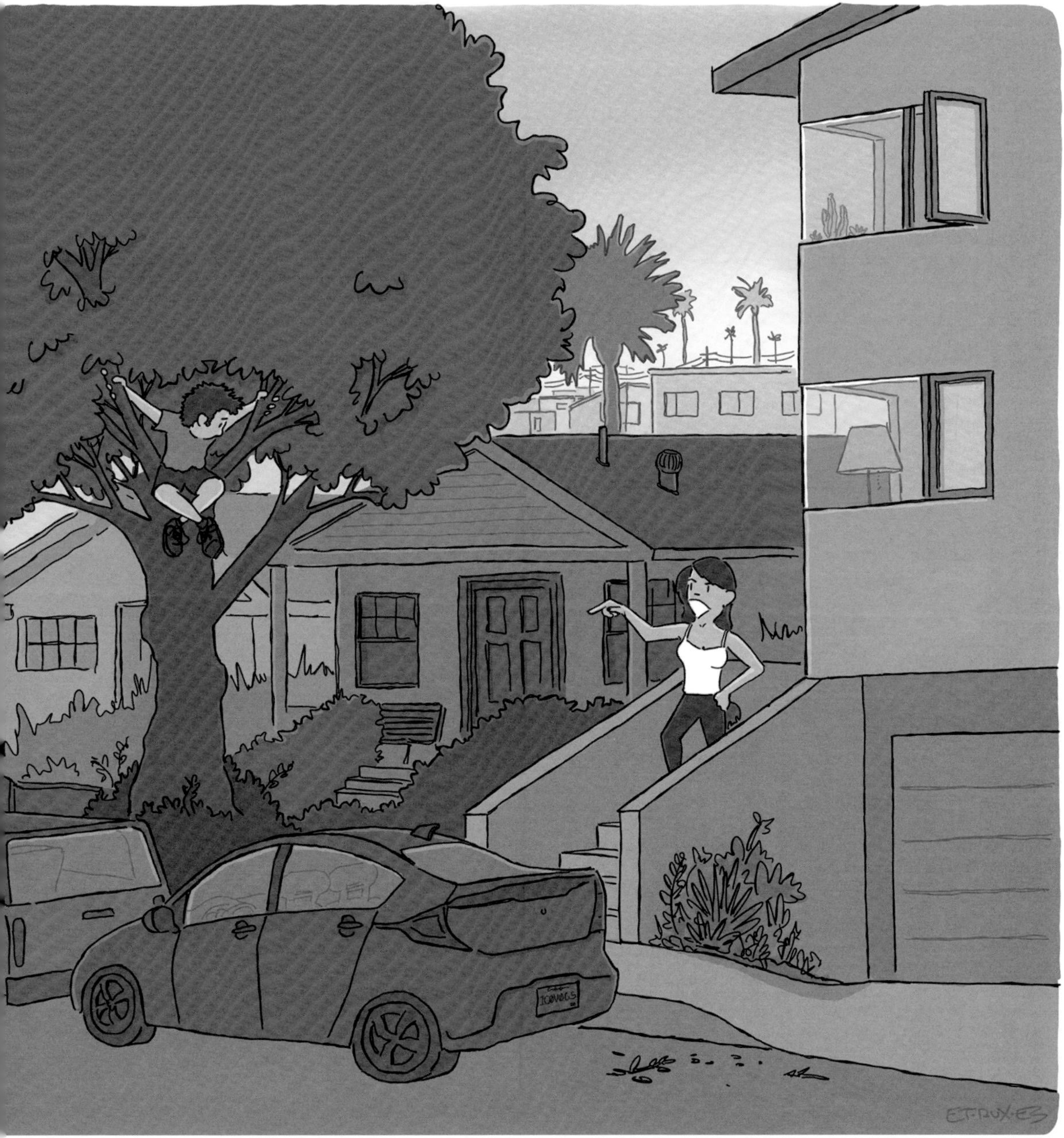

"Dad, why do ladies sometimes wear man buns?"

Gelson's. Silver Lake.

#RecencyBias

"Please make sure my dog, RuPaul, doesn't get any of those chips you're eating. He's vegan and gluten-free."

Party host. Silver Lake.

#RuPawl

Lady buying tiny Hawaiian shirt: "I'm turning our dog into a douchebag."

The Dog Bakery. The Farmers' Market. The Grove.
#alohound

Kid: Mommy always brings the reusable shopping bags from home.

Dad: She also takes 30-minute showers and drives a Range Rover. I love the Earth more.

Trader Joe's. Redondo Beach.

#baggage

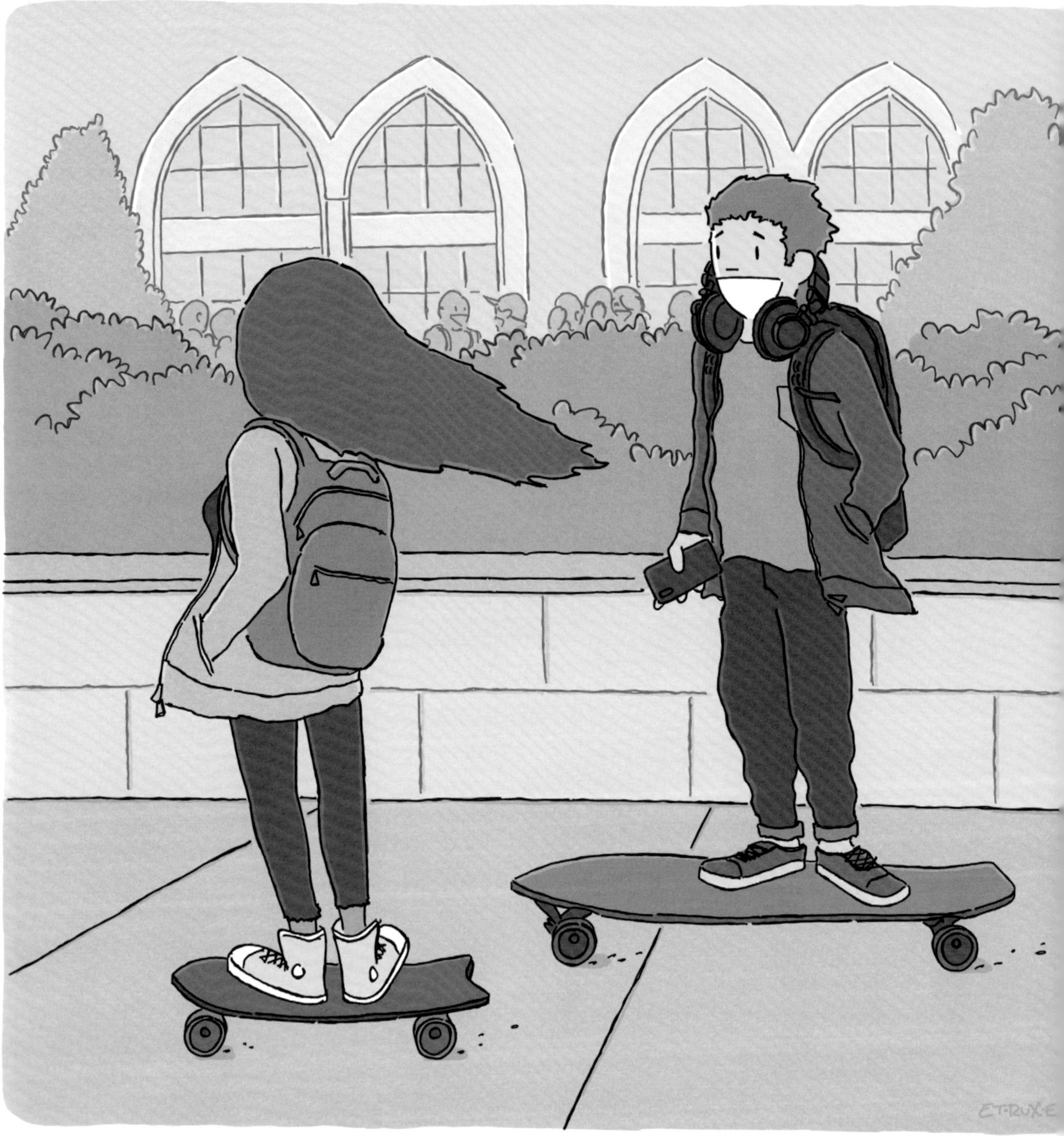
ET-RUX-E

"My parents would kill me if they knew they were spending $40K a year for me to take 'Intro to DJs.'"

Little girl: I'm scared.

Woman: What are you scared of?

Little girl: I'm scared our private jet won't have popcorn tomorrow.

Marina Del Rey.
#PopCulture #RelatableContent

Kids playing "make-believe" in line:

5-year-old: I can't have the peanut butter here because it has gluten and dairy in it.

3-year-old: Yeah, I can't have the chocolate because it's not *bahganic.*

Target. Eagle Rock.

#Gee-Mm-Ohs

Kid: Mom, I don't want to!

Mom: Riley, if you don't take this selfie with us, I will take away your drone.

Il Fornaio. Beverly Hills.
#DroneSelfie #FamilyCircus

"When you're a kid, your parents can see you naked, but strangers can't. When you're an adult, strangers can see you naked, but your parents can't. Circle of life."

Gjusta. Venice.
#NakedLunch

"Go hide and just text
me when you're ready!"

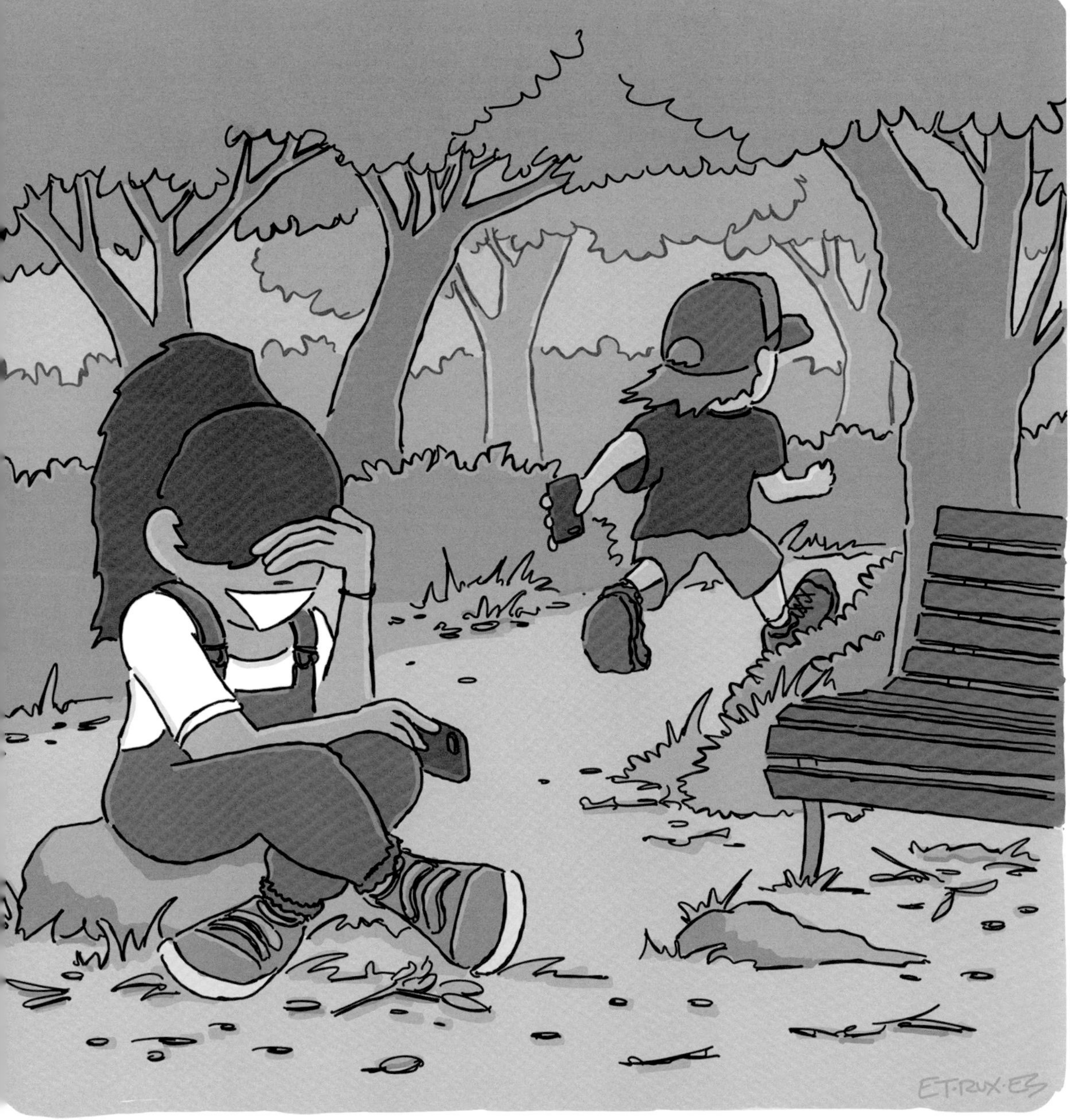

Woman to hairstylist:

"How much for my daughter's blow job?"

Hair Salon. Beverly Hills.

#JustBlowIt

Dad talking about his toddler:
"My kid is gonna think Third Eye Blind is classic rock."

Tiago. Hollywood.

#HowsItGonnaBe

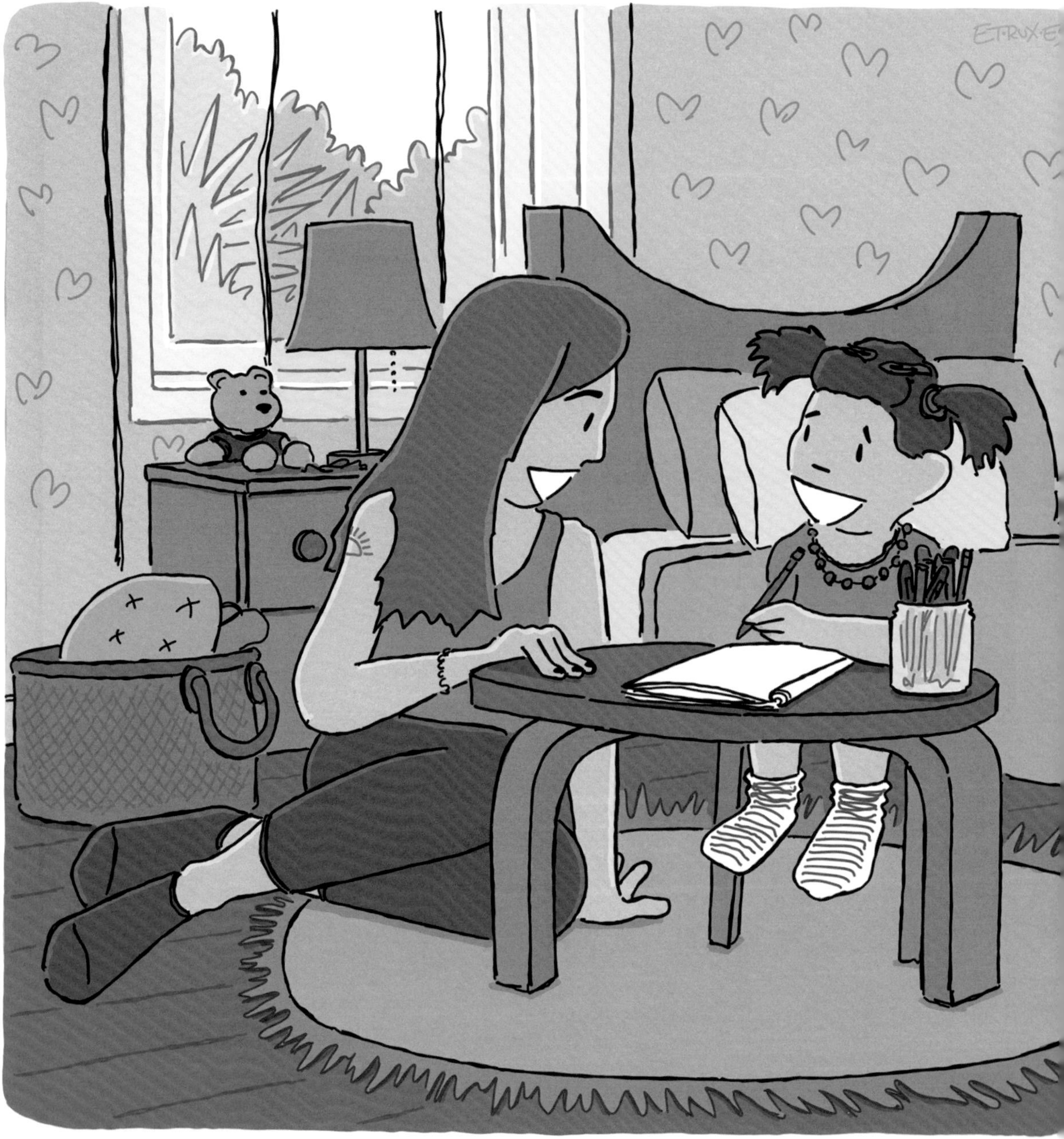

Nanny: Where does milk come from?

Toddler: Almonds!

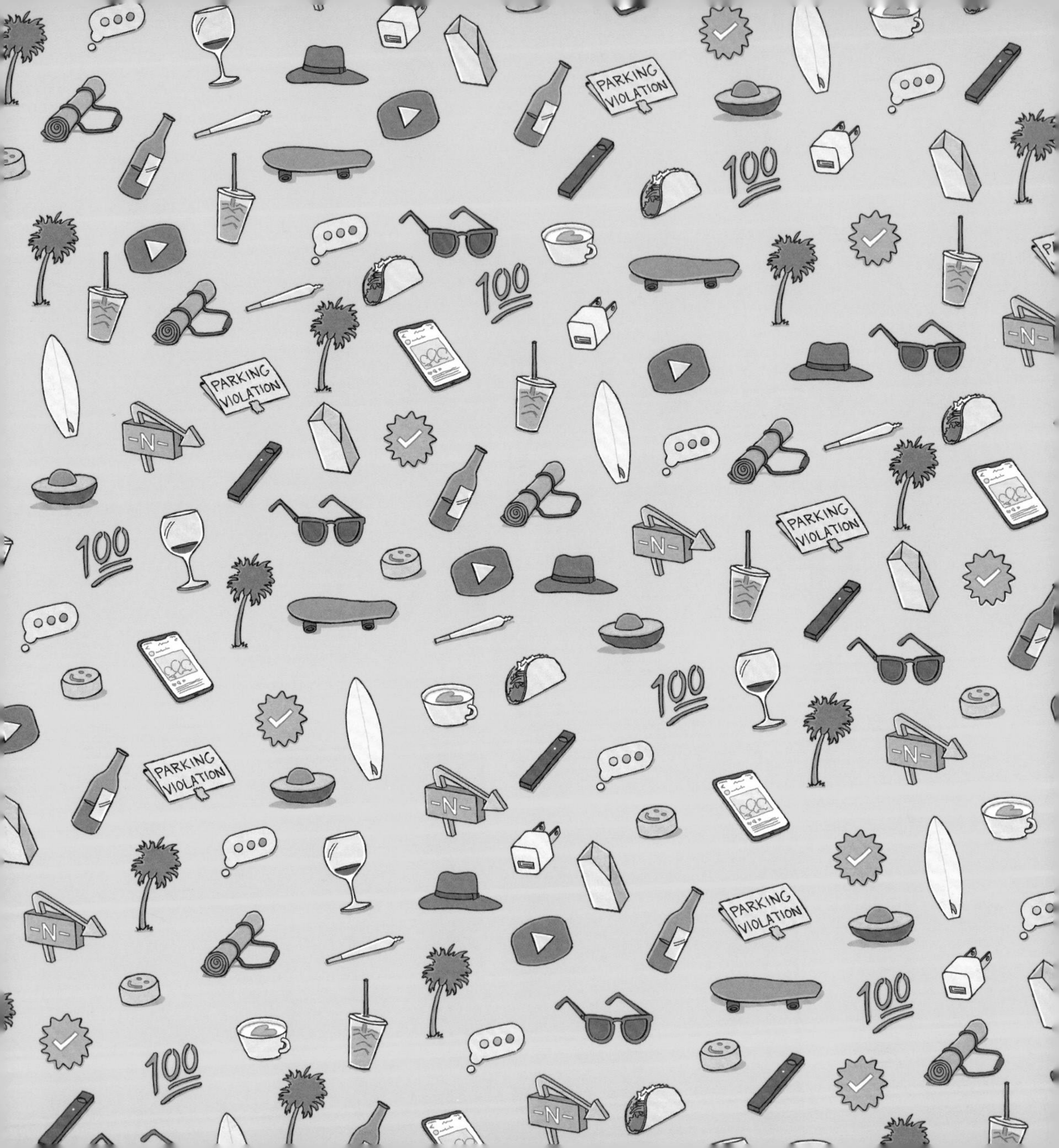
PARKING VIOLATION
100
N

#NIGHTLIFE AND PARTYING

Girl: What did we take the last time we went to Palm Springs?

Guy: Shrooms then Molly.

Girl: No, like, which freeway did we take?

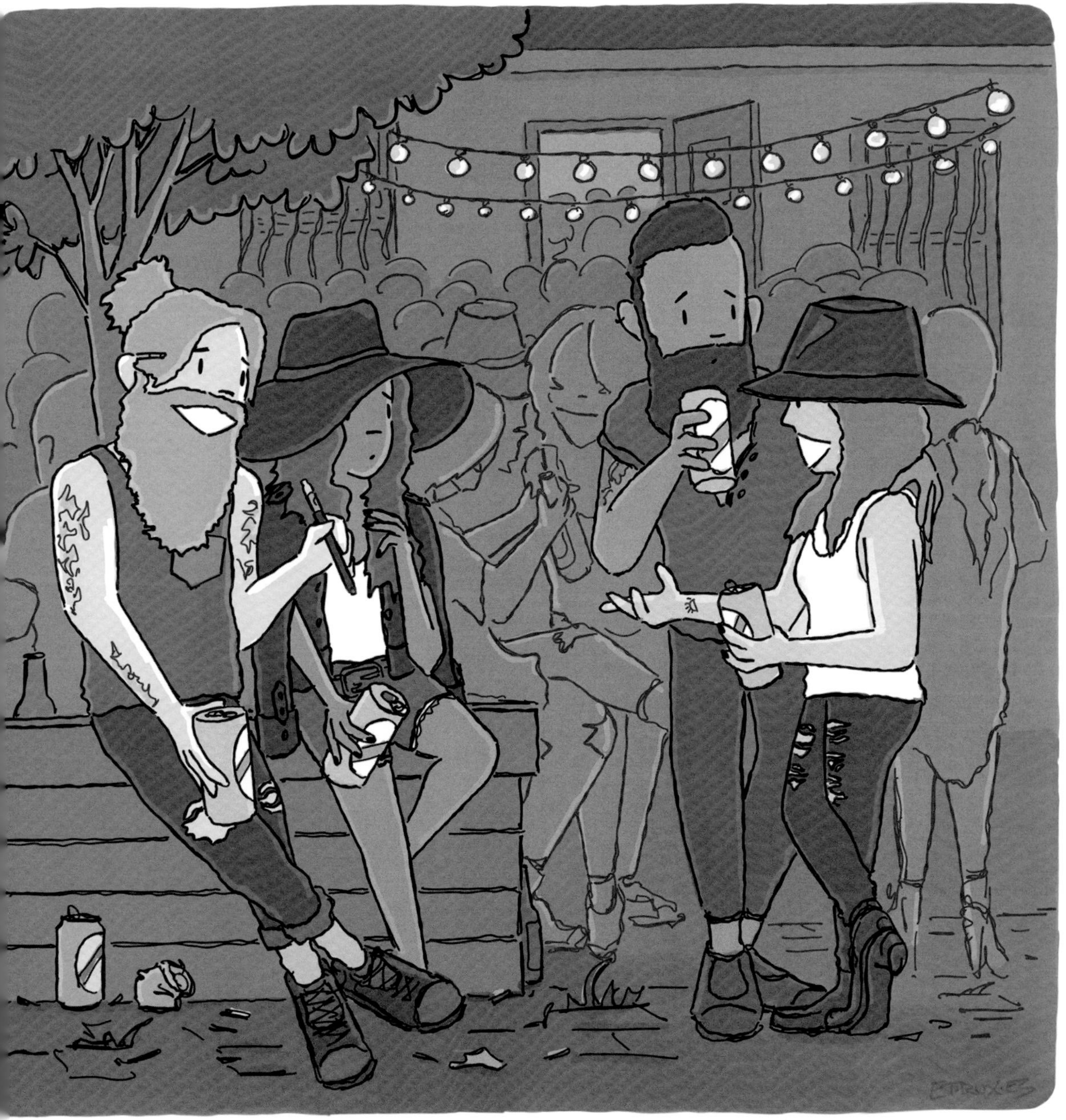

"L.A. is so weird. Everyone is like, 'Oh, cocaine on Sunday …juice cleanse and yoga and gratitude on Monday.'"

Cafe Gratitude. Larchmont.

#BothSidesNow

"This guy just bought me a drink at the bar and then he asked me to Venmo him."

E.P & L.P.

#StayClassy

Girl at bar, ordering a drink: It's 5 o'clock somewhere . . .

Friend: Yeah, it's 5 o'clock here . . . bitch, are you okay?"

Bouncer: Sleeveless shirt guy is a no-go.

Sleeveless shirt guy: I'm wearing $800 Pradas and you're worried about my lack of sleeves?

Outside of Doheny Room.

#BareArms

Girl: Can I get a glass of champagne?

Waiter: Can I see your ID?

Girl: I actually left my ID at home, but I can show you the Insta I posted on my 21st birthday in Vegas.

Nobu. Malibu.

#ProofOfLife

Bartender: Would you like to close your tab?

Drunk guy: A Lannister always pays his debts.

Cafe Habana. Malibu.

#BlondAmbition

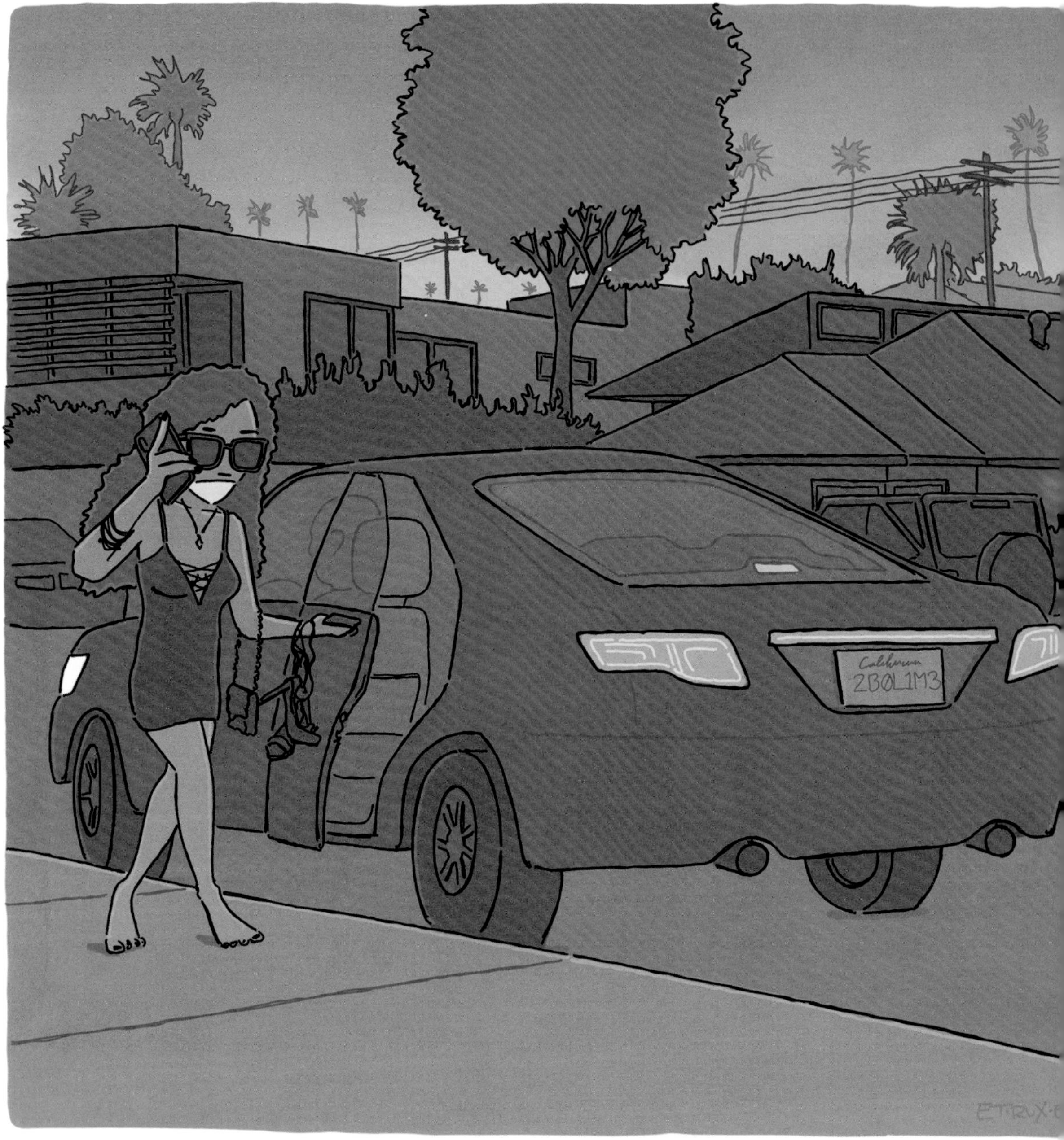
2B0L1M3

"The amount of coke he gave me did not equal the amount of head I gave him."

"I don't remember much from last night, but I had three missed calls from a contact saved as 'Tattoo Face Bootsy Bellows Do Not Answer.'"

Tasting Kitchen. Venice.

#MorningAfterPhil #DigitalHangover

"Dude, you got drunk and ran down the street naked."

"I wasn't naked. I had condoms on my feet."

House Party. Long Beach.
#RubberMeetsTheRoad #AirJohnson

"OMG! I can see the disco lights pouring through your thigh gap."

"Yeah, I'm not eating."

"That's so good."

House Party. Hollywood Hills.
#MindTheGap

Drunk guy emerging out of nowhere: Marco!

Friends: Polo!

Drunk guy: No, no, Marco is my Uber driver.

Mar Vista.
#DrinkingGames

Drunk Girl 1: Where do you live?

Drunk Girl 2: I live $10 away.

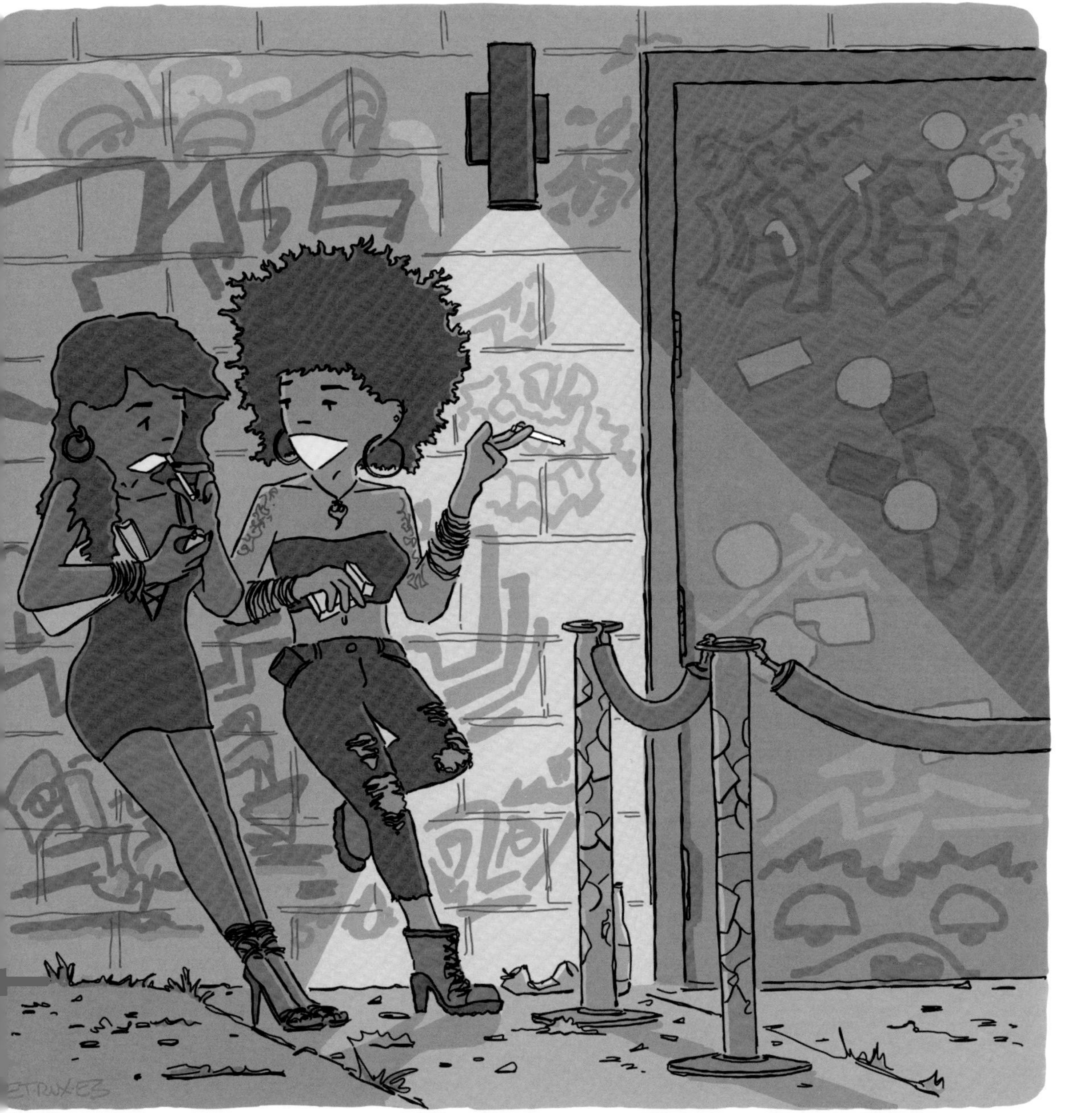

"If I could get back the lost time
I've spent playing Candy Crush,
I would have graduated by now."

"You would also have to get back
all the brain cells you've lost
snorting MDMA."

Hyperion Public.

#Crushing

Listening to Jewel:

"I love this song; it makes me want to relapse."

Sunset Tower.

#YodelingAndTidePods

"He's in my phone as 'Dad,' so when the cops got there, they called him first. It was awkward for everyone."

No Vacancy. Hollywood.

#FathersDay

Uber driver: My girlfriend lives 8,000 miles away and I've never cheated on her.

Passenger: That must be tough.

Uber driver: Yeah, but I have a ho for emotional support.

Santa Monica Blvd.
#ESH

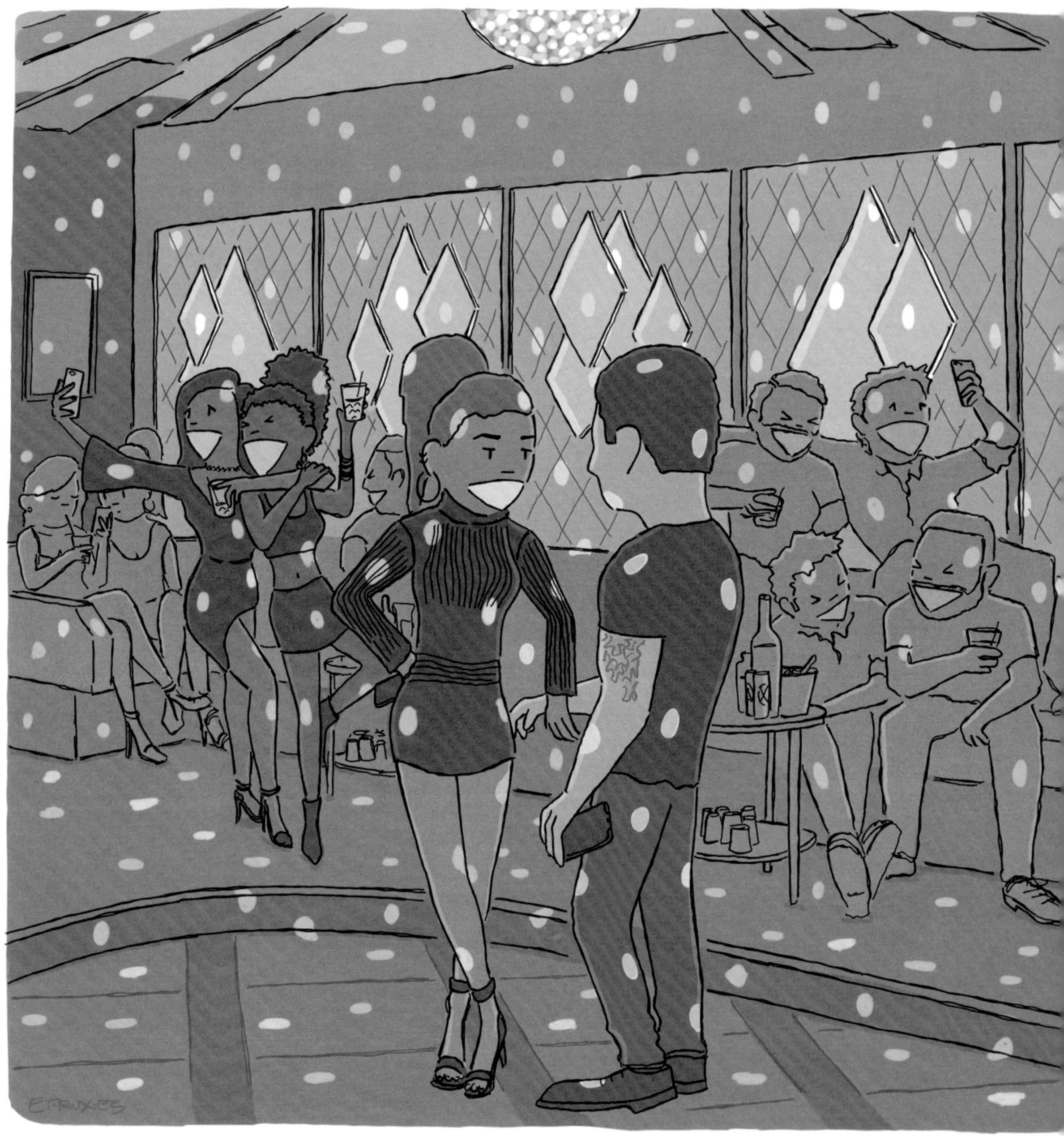

"Why can't I be a vehement feminist who also listens to trap music?"

"Why did you friend zone him?"

"He tried to order a vodka soda with his Harry Potter wand."

Buffalo Club.
#MagicTrick

"What should I do with my fake ID?"

"Bury it so that 100 years from now our descendants will know the struggle of being 20 but having to look 27 in order to have a beer."

USC.
#TimeCapsule

Girl 1: I drunkenly made plans to go to the doctor with this girl last night.

Girl 2: That's like brunch for 30-year-olds.

Good Girl Dinette. Highland Park.
#HangoverCures

Guy 1, yelling: I hope Uber surges on you!

Guy 2, yelling back: I drove here, bitch!

Playhouse. Hollywood Blvd.

#SurgeProtector

"The best is yet to come."

"I've only ever felt that right
before the edibles kick in."

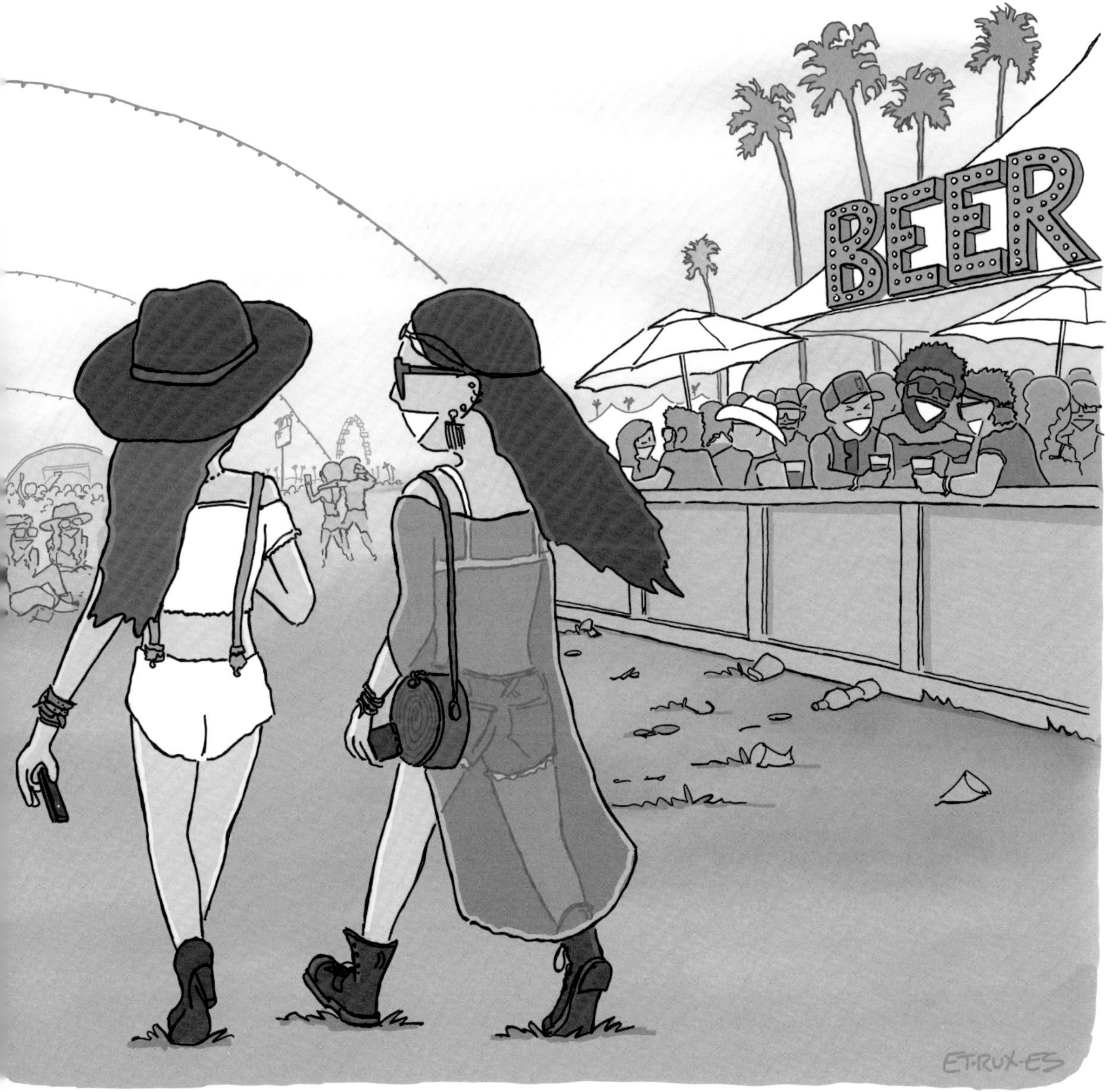
BEER
E.T.RUX.ES

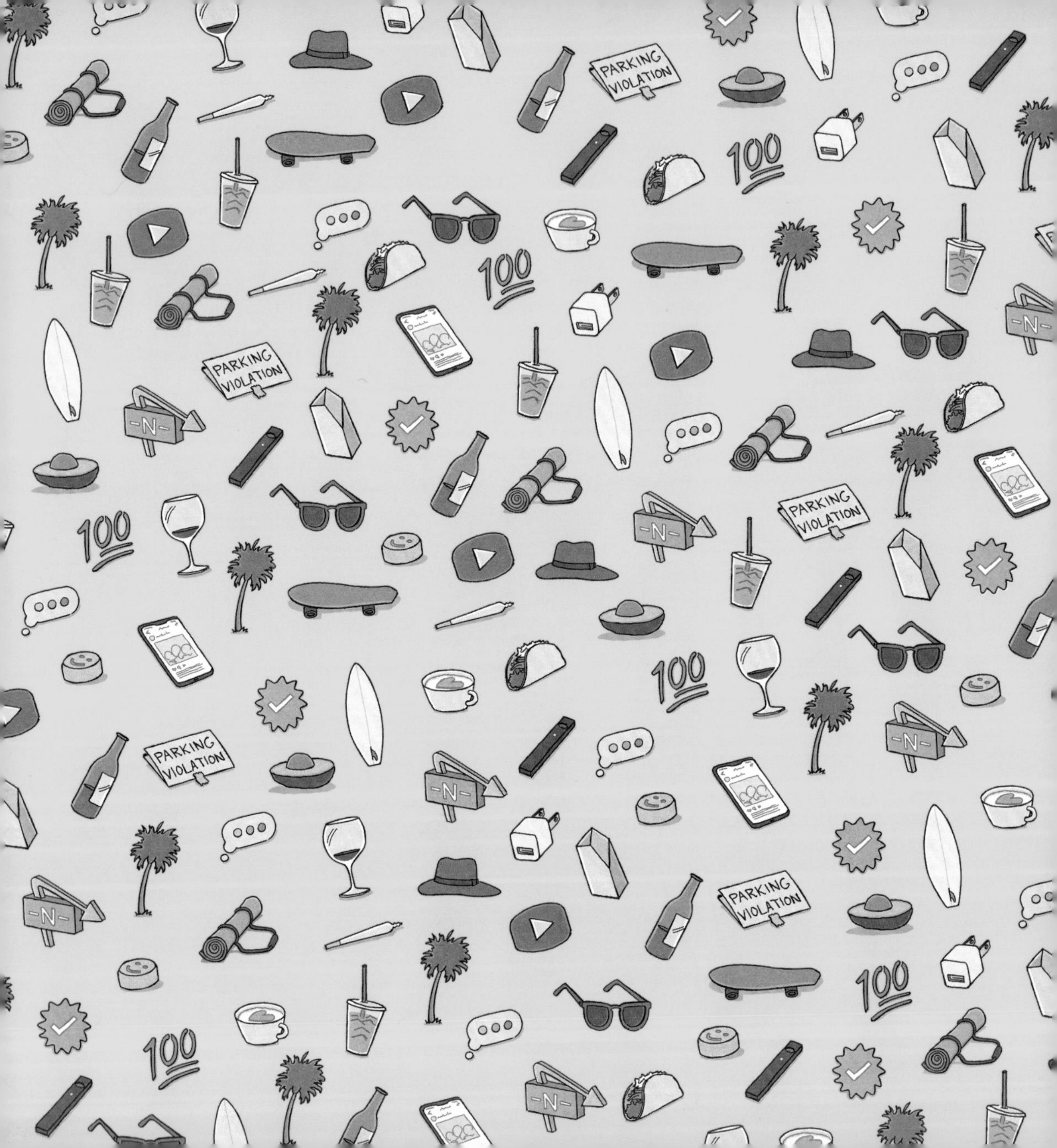
PARKING VIOLATION
PARKING VIOLATION
PARKING VIOLATION
PARKING VIOLATION
PARKING VIOLATION
100
100
100
100
100
100
-N-
-N-
-N-
-N-
-N-
-N-
-N-

#DIGITAL_LIFE

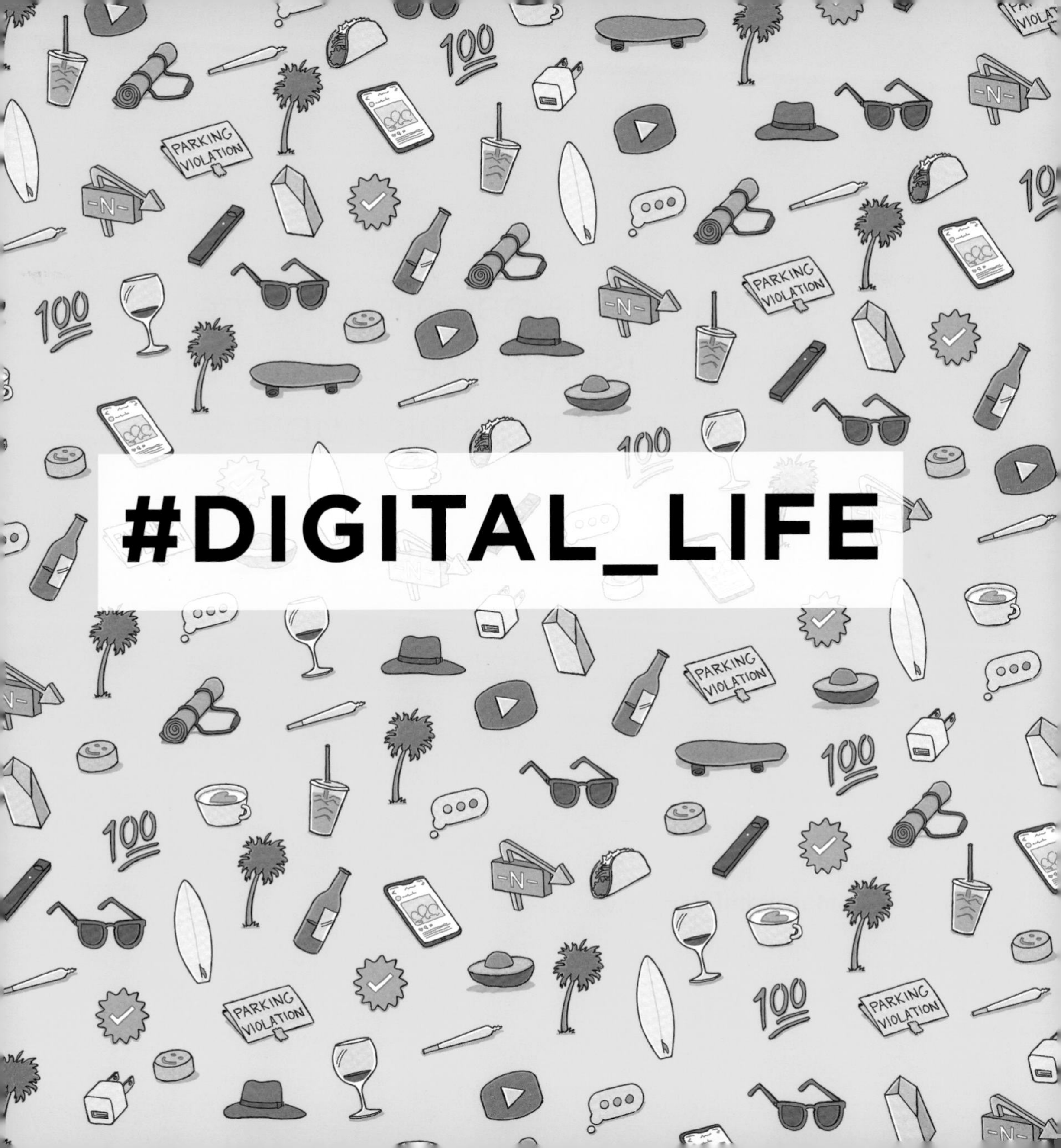
PARKING VIOLATION
100
-N-

"My whole life people told me not to trust strangers. Now all of a sudden they pick up my laundry, drive me around while I'm wasted, and bring me ramen."

Murakami. Melrose.

#NewNormal

"No, I don't want to eat; I only came to L.A. with you to take some damn cute Insta photos. Where's that stupid pink wall everyone goes to?"

In line. Starbucks. L.A. Live.
#InstaTourism #TearDownThatWall

Girl: I want cereal, do you want some?

Checks fridge

Ugh, there's no milk left.

Alexa: Adding milk to your shopping list.

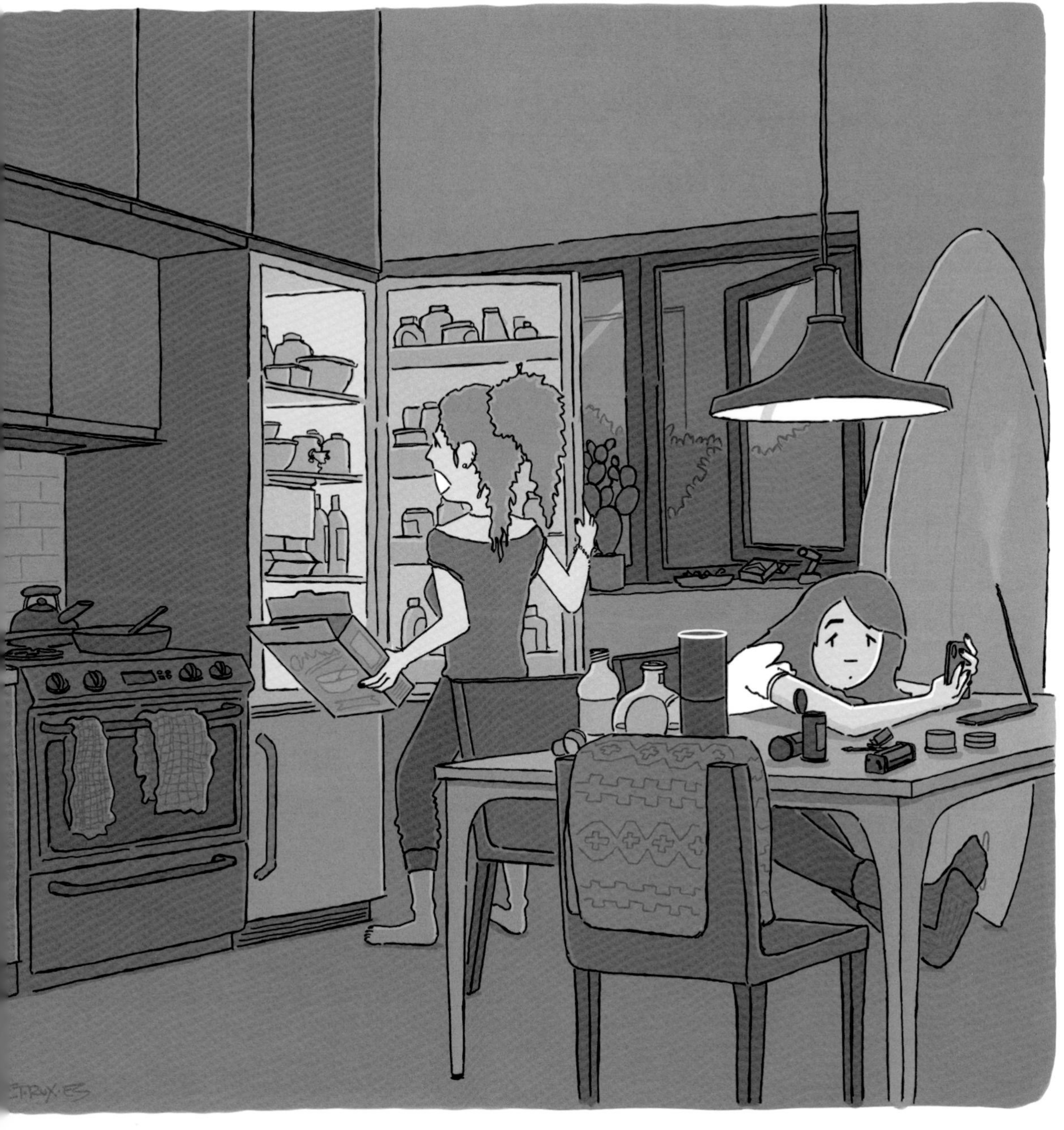

"She's got 34,000 Instagram followers. There were three people at her birthday dinner."

Pace. Laurel Canyon.

#LonelyButPopular

"One man's TBT is another man's PTSD."

In line. Whole Foods. DTLA.

#PastLivesMatter

"I just asked her what she did and she responded, 'I am' . . . She doesn't have iMessage, so I don't know if she's in the middle of her sentence or if that was her answer."

Sushi Park. Sunset Blvd.

#ExistentialTexts

"Nothing screams of desperation like a paragraph of hashtags."

North Hollywood.

#actor #model #ScenePartnerSundays #grateful #gratitude #GrapefruitAttitude #SpritualJourneyCapableWomanRoaring #RicardStraus #HesAComposer #MaybeIShouldWriteMusic #AlmostFamousIsAGoodMovie #ImAlmostFamousKindOf #YogurtIsMySpiritAnimal #WasStBartsARealSaint? #HeMustHaveBeenRich #SpiritualButSexy #TulumTuesdays #ImWritingAWebSeriesWithMyBestie #WTFIsWrongWithUsHumanBeings

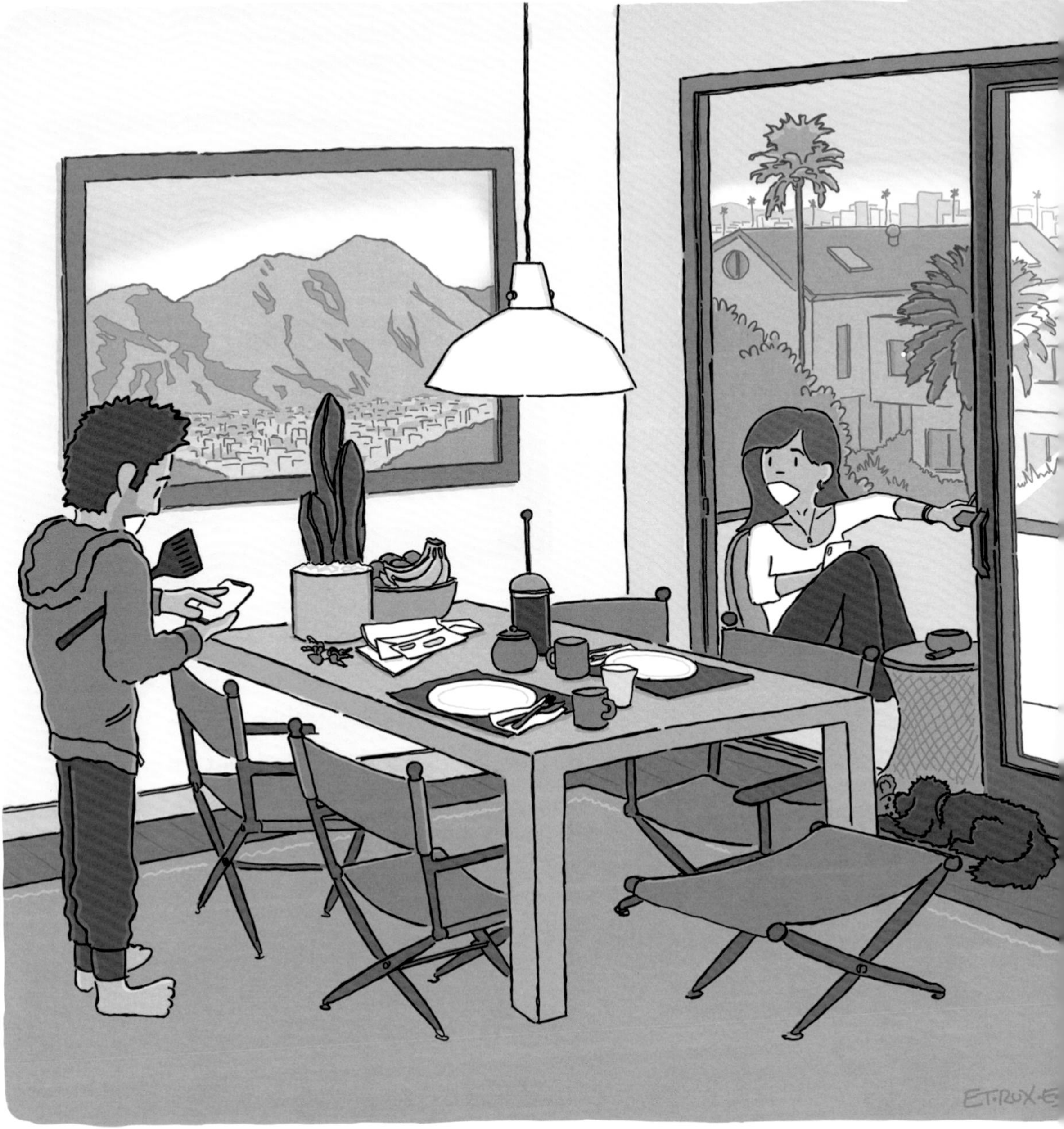

Guy: Fuck, I got hacked!

Girl: Bank or Instagram?

Guy: Bank.

Girl: Oh, thank God.

"I remember the old days when you needed a degree and a resume to get a job. Now you need 10,000 followers and a mediocre blog."

Tsujita Annex.

#SelfieMajor

"Ew! You have read receipts?
I hate those."

"I'm trying to live a more
authentic life."

Aussie Pie Kitchen. Santa Monica.

#BeTheChange

"Ugh, fuck social media . . . We weren't meant to know what some skinny girl in Australia is doing with her life."

Bricks and Scones.

#DigitalDetox

"He asked me how my day was, and I told him to just watch my Instagram Story."

Manhattan Beach.

#episodes

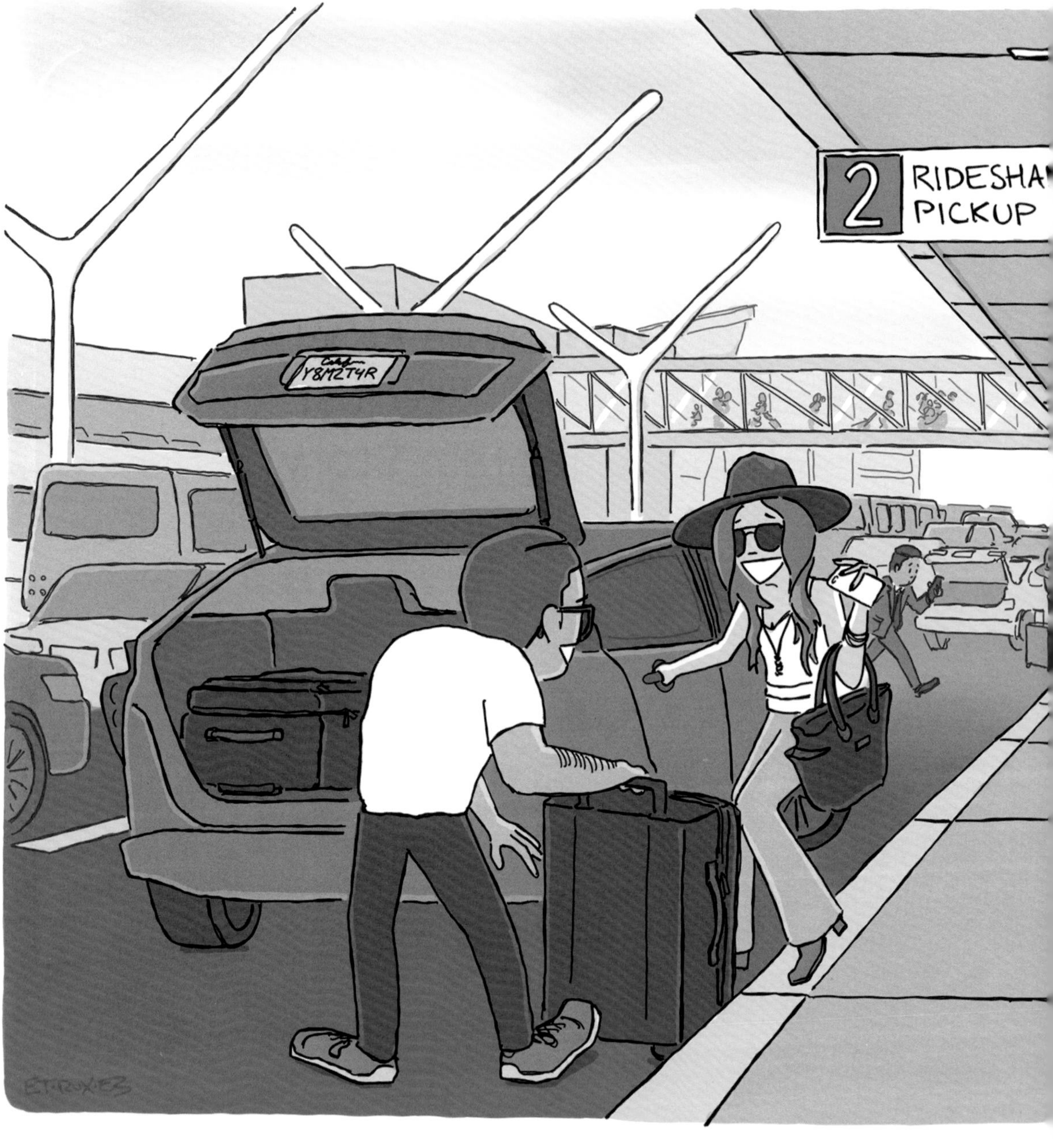
2
RIDESHA
PICKUP
Y8M2T4R

Guy: And what brought you to L.A.?

Girl: I came here to work on my Instagram.

At Amazon Books: "Remember when stores built websites? Now websites are building stores."

Westfield. Century City.

#webSITES

"No one's trying to get married here. Between porn and Postmates, humans don't even need each other anymore."

Copa Vida, Pasadena.

**Hopefully, you find someone who will stay with you when Instagram is dead and your kids are grown up and wearing real-life digital face filters on Bumble dates in a virtual-reality Westworld-style theme park and communicating in emoji squeaks instead of words.

#PornMates

"I can't believe we've lived to see cyberstalking become romantic . . . Maybe next we'll destigmatize sliding into someone's DMs."

New Yorker. Chateau Marmont.

#DestigMatize

At the mall: "I bought stuff online while I was waiting for you to shop."

Westfield Topanga.

#presale

Guy 1: Yo I called you last night, why didn't you pick up?

Guy 2: Dude, you know I don't use my phone for that.

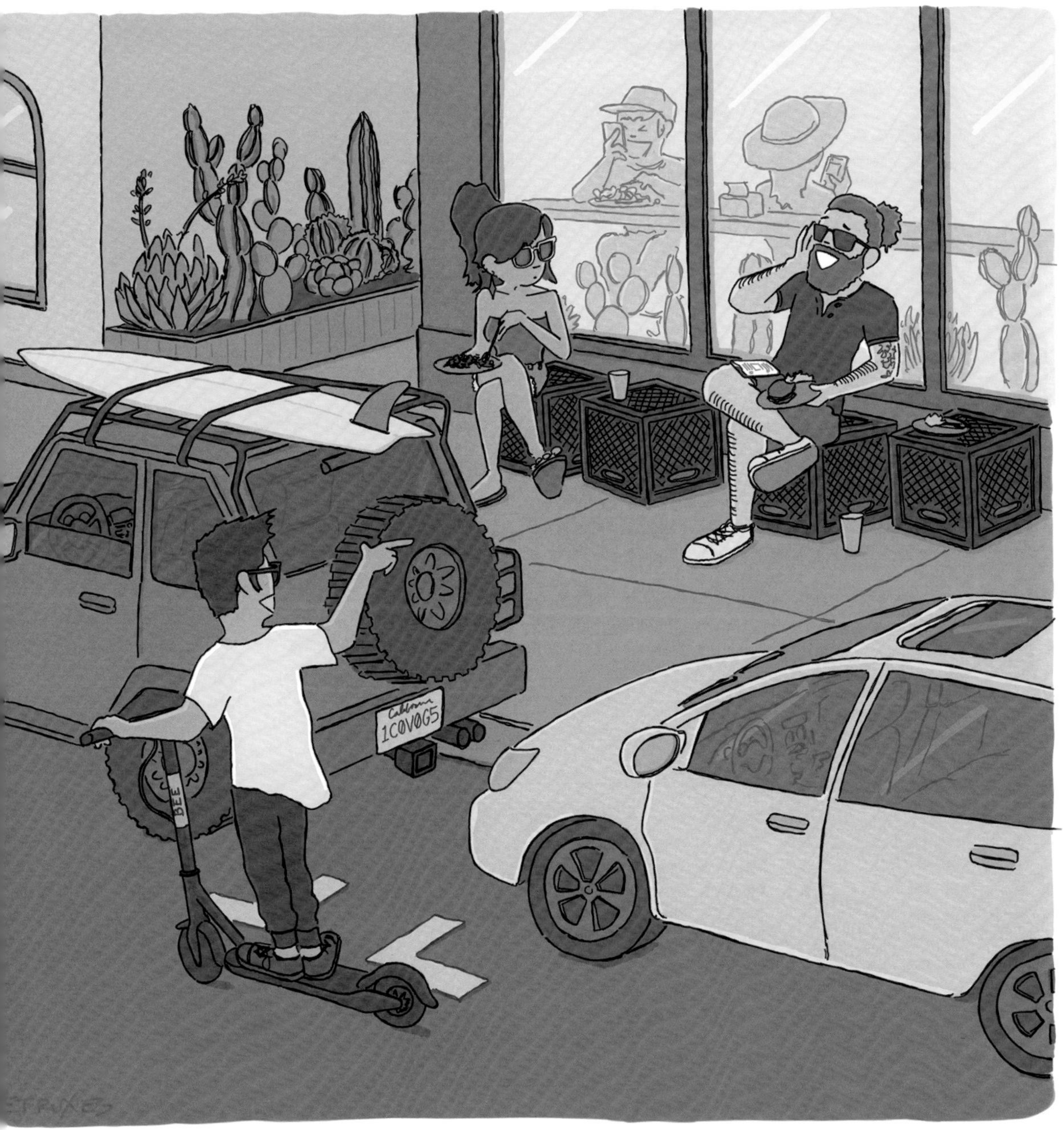
California
1C0V0G5
BEE

"There was literally an orgy happening in his bathroom, and we were talking about cryptocurrency in the kitchen."

West L.A.

#BlockChainGangBang

"I want someone to do a real, unfiltered Snapchat story. Only the *real shit*. Walking to the ATM and seeing you don't have any cash. Not getting into the club. Not being able to get it up. Relatable stuff."

Blue Bottle.

#DocuSnap

"He's verified . . . on Twitter."

"Everyone is. I know people in prison who are verified on Twitter."

Party. Baldwin Hills.

#CheckMate

"I got so high the other night, I listened to a podcast on double speed . . . and I understood it."

Good Housekeeping HLP.
#MindHacker

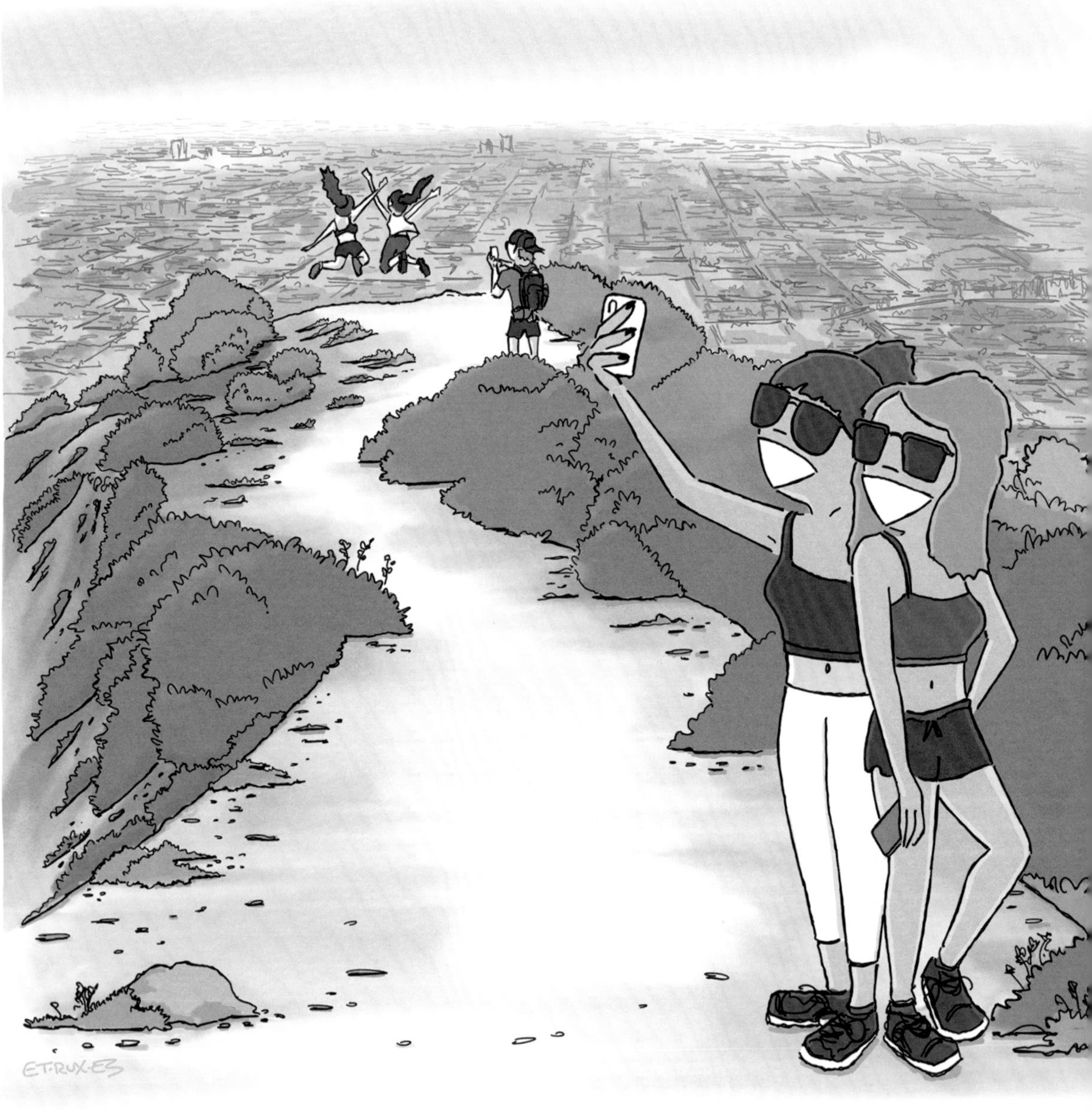

ET·RUX·E3

"Ugh, you're in my light!"

"I AM your light, bitch."

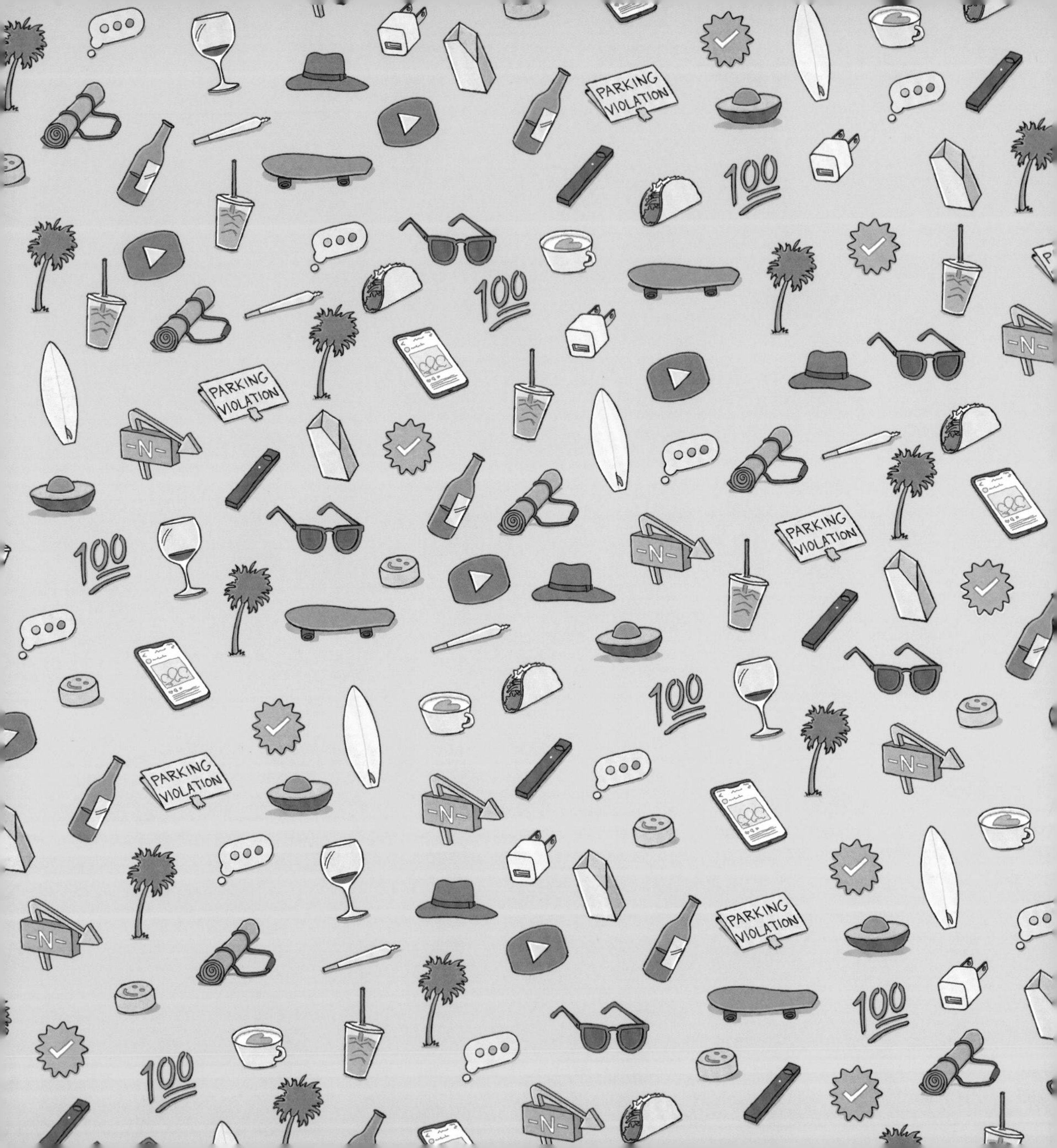
PARKING VIOLATION
100
-N-

#ONLY_IN_LA

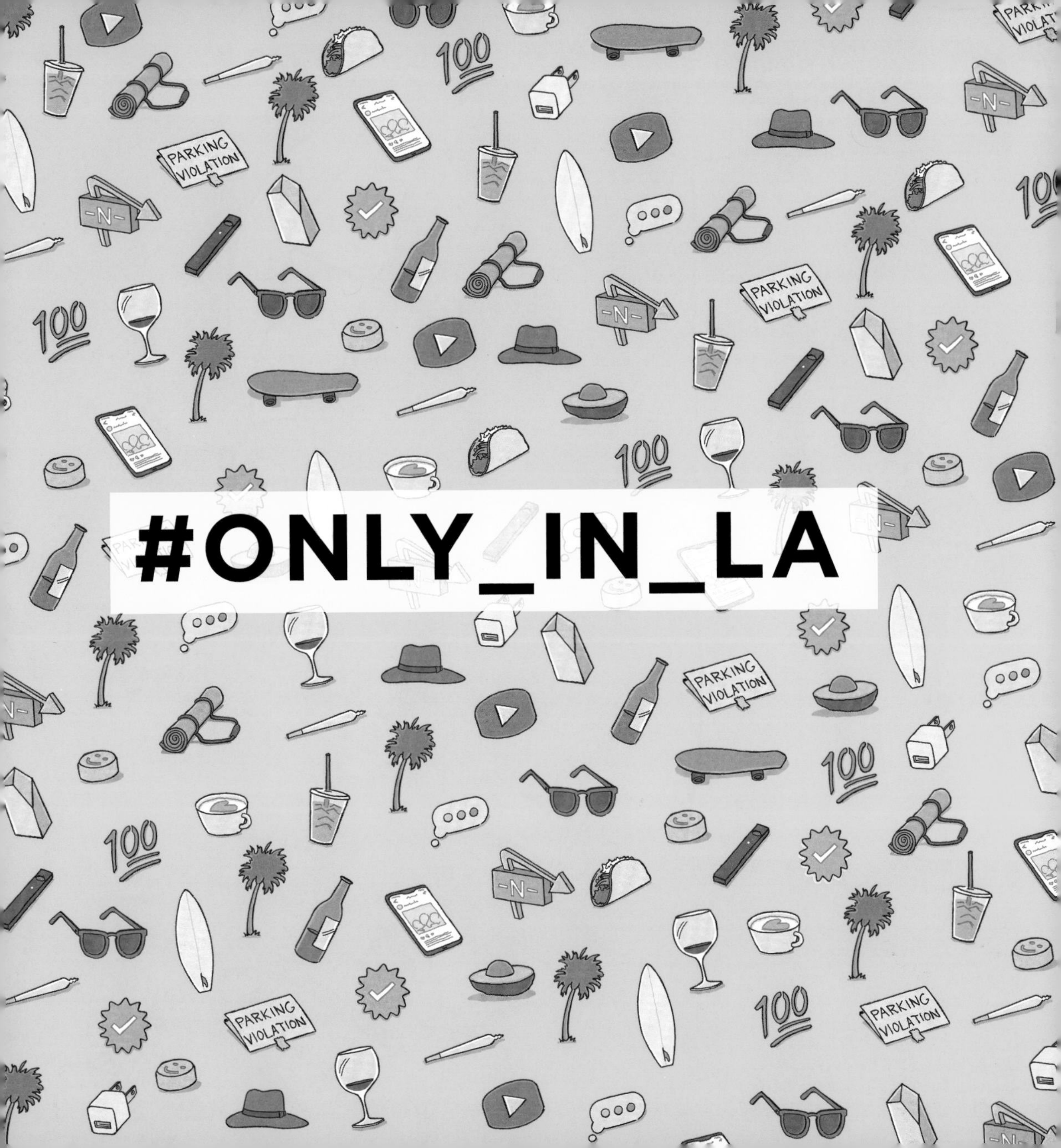
PARKING VIOLATION
100

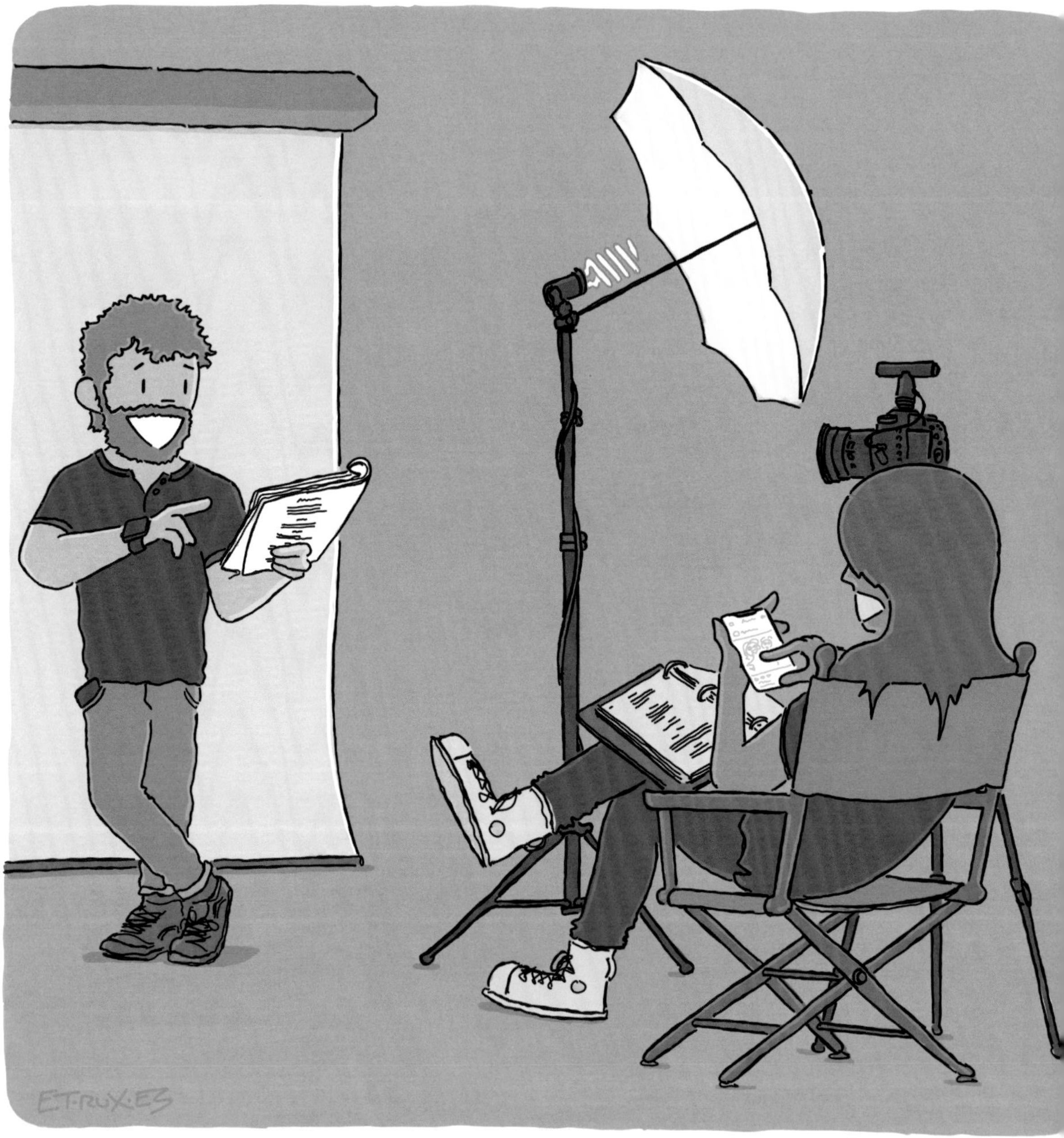
ET·RUX·ES

"Can I also read for the role of Kale?"

"Do you have a man bun?"

"No, I just cut mine off."

"Sorry, Kale has a man bun."

Woman: Is it going to be a turbulent flight? I wanna know if I should pop a Xanax?

Flight attendant: Probably not, but I'd pop it anyways.

JetBlue flight to L.A.

#PreparationX

"Has he got a lot of money?"

"I'm not sure. He drives a Prius.
I can't tell."

Sugarfish. La Brea.

#YouAreWhatYouDrive

"The thing I hate about Daylight Savings is that I look really fucking good in sunglasses, and now that it gets dark at 4:00, I have so much less time to wear them."

All Saints. Beverly Hills.

#CoreyHart

"Of course L.A. is a tough place to live. It's a city full of people who were too good for their own hometowns."

Intelligentsia. Silver Lake.

#HometownHotties #BeautyQueensAndQuarterbacks

"Lately, the only way I can fall asleep is by mentally making a list of people I would thank in an acceptance speech."

Emmys Viewing Party. Sherman Oaks.

#IWantToThankMyHolisticDentistWhoNeverChasedMe
DownForThe2KIStillOweHim #MyPaleoChefsCousin
#MyFirstBoyfriendWhoStuckByMeUntilIGotFamous
ThenICheatedOnHimWithaBroodingActorWhileOnSetIn
Vancouver #DrTattoff

"The traffic on the 10 is so bad in the morning . . . My friend brings her vibrator with her in the car. She says she usually gets off at around Cloverfield. I'm thinking about trying it."

Bassike. Venice.

#HandsFree #HighVibes

Cosmetologist: Let's take a look at these wrinkles.

Patient: You mean my experience stripes?

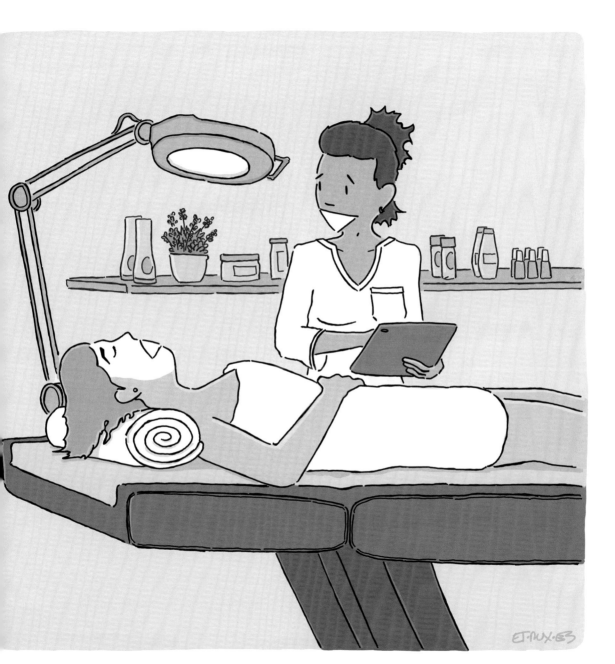

"The word *bougie* comes from the word *bourgeois*."

"But bourgeois means middle class?"

"Yeah, but the middle class was lit back then."

Bean Town. Sierra Madre.
#MiddleSchooled

Guy: Are these shirts bisexual?

Salesperson: You mean unisex?

Gift Shop. Hermosa Beach Pier.

#ReversibleTop

"Every new friend I make is another person who might ask me to drive them to LAX in the future. And I don't need that."

Son of a Gun.

#NoNewFriends

Angry customer: Do you know who I am?!

Cashier: Someone help this guy— he doesn't know who he is!

GTA. Venice.

#HipsterSartre

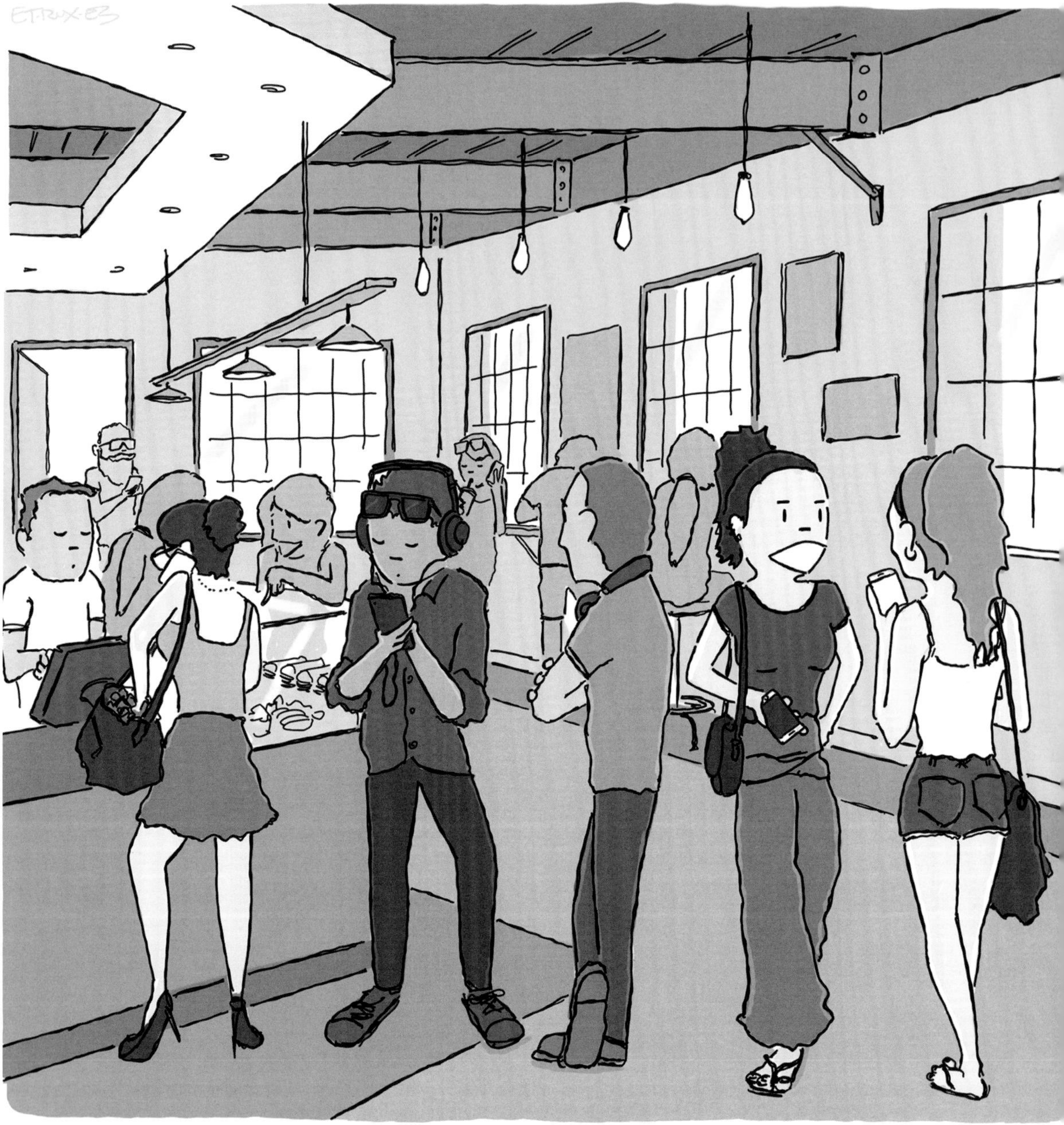

"She has 22,000 likes on a picture of a gourmet donut and I can't get anyone to read my script."

"It's weird how when you wear a bathrobe inside you look rich, but when you wear one outside you look poor."

Starbucks. Hollywood.

#RobeParadox

"I've been 'faking it 'til I make it' for so long I think I'm just fake now."

Pete's Coffee. Beverly Hills.

#MethodActor

"Do you think you'd be prepared for an earthquake?"

"I'm not even prepared for regular life."

Stumptown. DTLA.

#faulty

"Everyone in L.A. is in competition with each other to be the most spiritual or the most anxious."

Q Restaurant. DTLA.

#EdvardMunch #EdvardMonk

High school science teacher: "If you need to buy your Coachella tickets during class, that's okay."

Studio City.

#MusicClass

"It's so cold out I can't tell if people are breathing or vaping."

North Hollywood.
#PuffDaddy

"My agent keeps saying I look too slutty in all my pictures. Like, I can't help it. That's genetics."

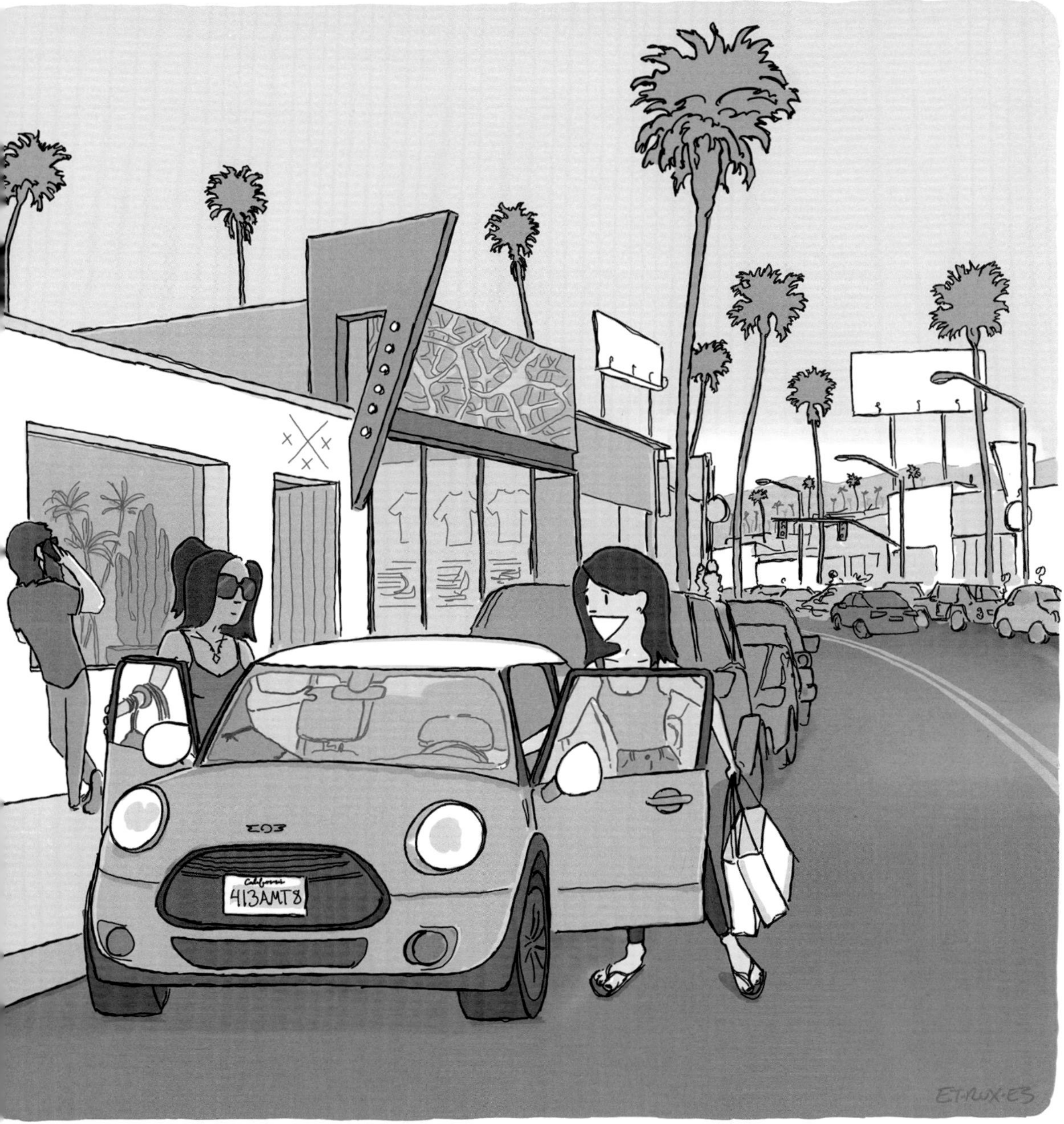
413AMT8

"What is gentrification?"

"It's when you have a kimono store and a kaftan store on the same street."

Abbot Kinney.
#AK247

"This afternoon I asked the woman doing my nails if she was mad at me. It's the most intimate relationship I currently have and I can't afford to fuck it up."

Trejos Tacos. Hollywood.

#HandJob

"He doesn't believe in money . . . He was, like, 'I'm post-economic.' It's easy to say that shit when you've sold your company for 20 million."

"Everyone else who's 'post-economic' is fucking homeless."

Loft Party. DTLA.

#Futurism #Realism

"Can I not just ONCE sit down for a cup of coffee in this town without having to overhear three guys brainstorm a time-travel movie?"

Verve. West 3rd Street.

#TheBadTimeline

"He can't make it to brunch because production on the movie is fitting him for a prosthetic wiener. He was going to go full frontal, but they said it didn't look great on camera."

Taste. Melrose.
#BodyDouble

"Have you done anything fun in Hollywood?"

"We got to see Ron Jeremy at CVS checking his blood pressure on the little machine."

Hollywood and Highland.

#PornStarHealthCare #UnderPressure

"I love Martin Luther King's 'I Dreamed a Dream' speech."

"That's *Les Mis*, you idiot."

The Abbey.
#CultureClub

"They're 24 and getting married and they can afford to buy a house? How?! I can't even afford a burrito in the three days leading up to each paycheck!"

House Party. Pasadena.

**Your high school sweetheart Ashton thinks Sugarfish is a Swedish candy, just bought a house in Boise, and has a newborn. You know the difference between kampachi and albacore but can't afford either. #MidwestMature

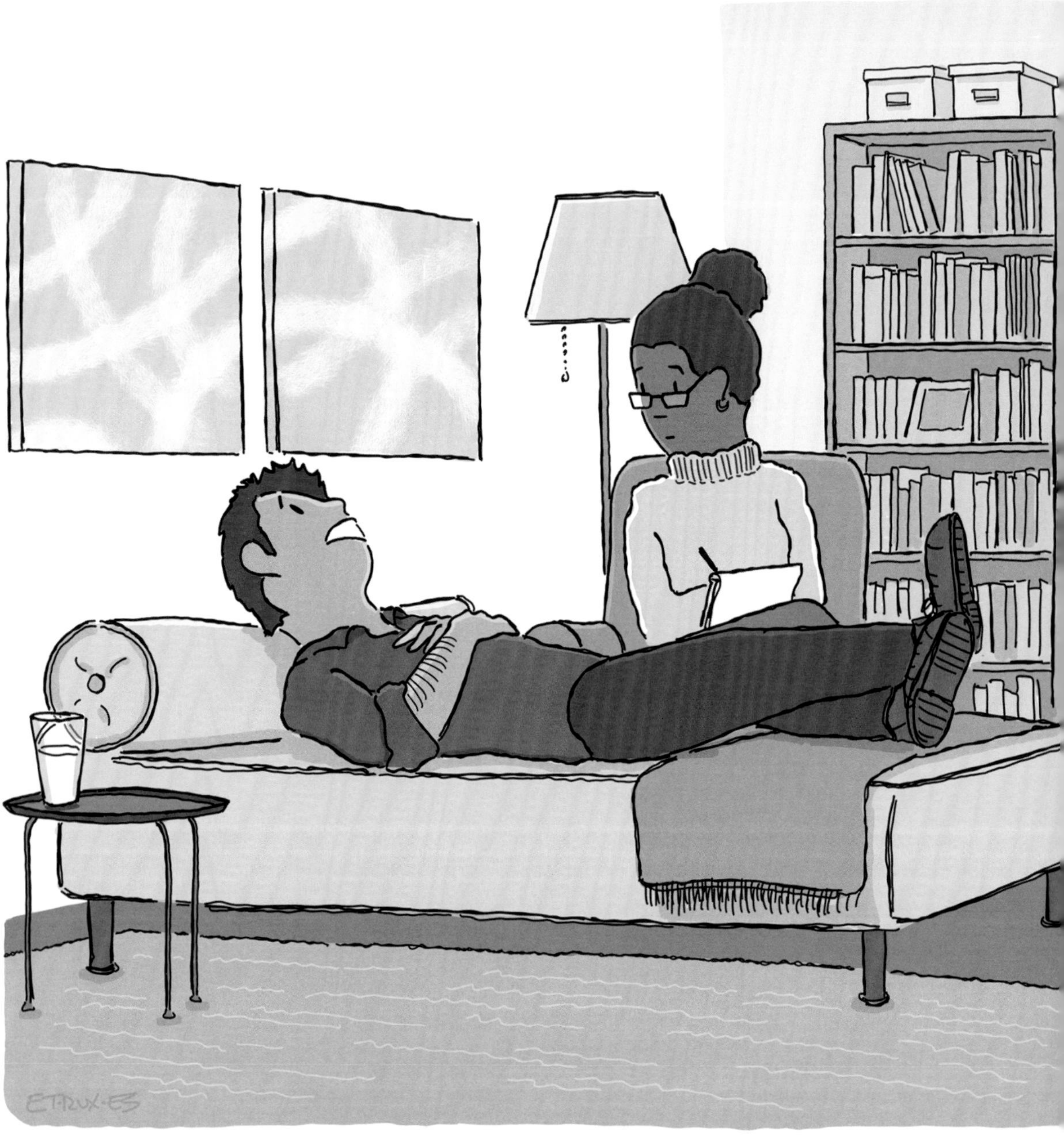

"Everyone in L.A. can see that my bullshit is bullshit . . . and I need to be with someone who finds my bullshit inspirational."

"We were at dinner and she fake-humbly mentioned she just got to 20,000 followers, so I said, 'Chill, I have a charming, little-shit 15-year-old cousin with 1.5 million. Life is about perspective.'"

Dinner Party. Playa Vista.
#RelativesAndRelativity

"I had only one line."

"Wait, are we talking about
coke or acting?"

Party. Venice.
#BlurredLines

"I'm having the worst week.
My hairdresser broke up with me.
He sent me a text message that
said, 'I'm sorry, but I don't think
I can help you or give you what
you want anymore. Happy hair.'"

SAG Screening. Director's Guild.

#FinalCut

Guy: What's the code for the bathroom?

Barista: 2007.

Guy: Oh, the year of our Lord and Savior, Britney Spears.

Verve. DTLA.
#StarSigns

"First it's pilot season, then awards season, now it's festival season. I feel like L.A. just creates seasons to make up for the fact that we don't have actual seasons."

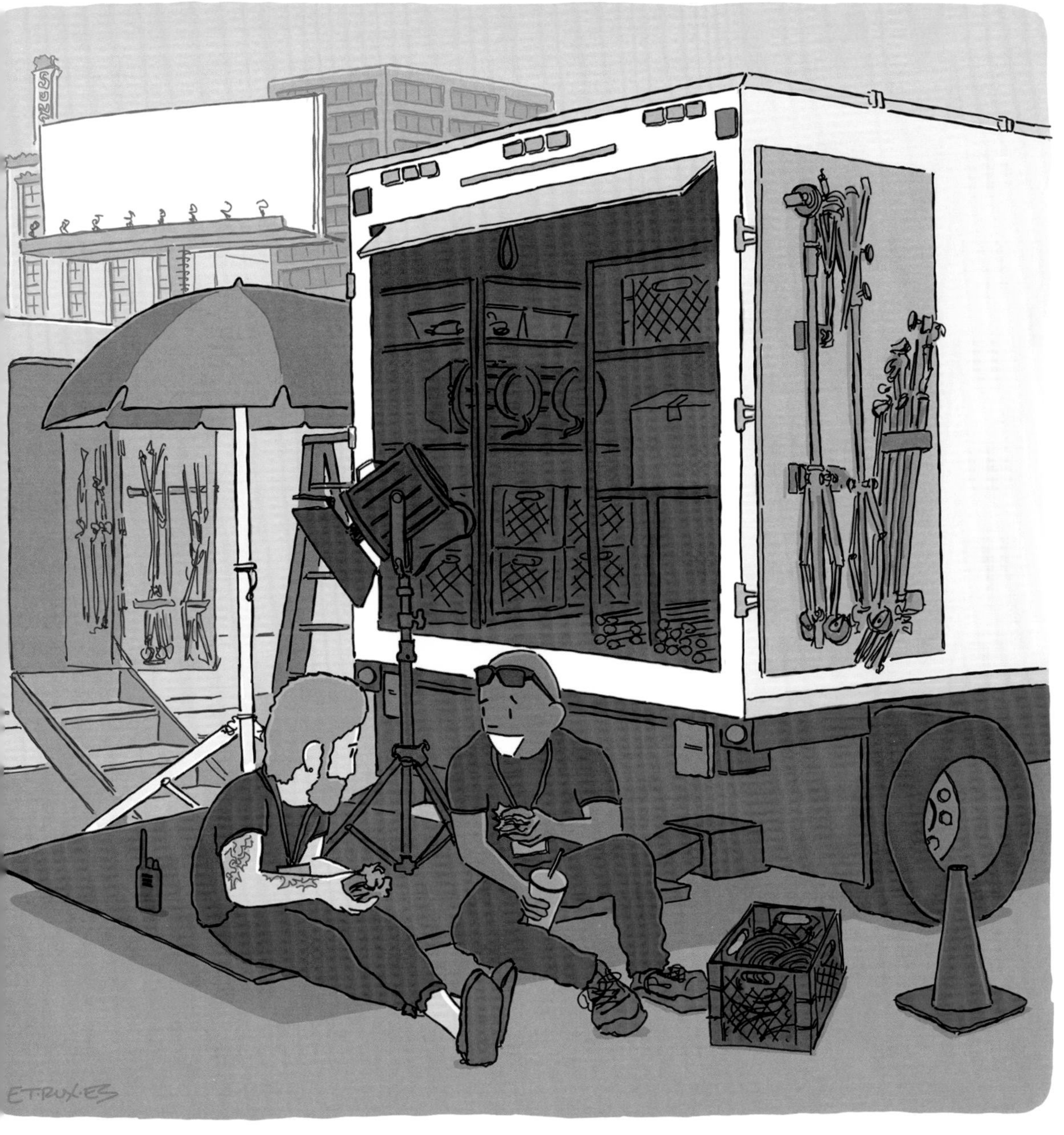

Woman: I'm hungry.

Man: Hashtag me too?

Woman: Hashtag nope.

Griffith Park.

#YouNot

Girl holding a copy of La Bible in French:

"What's an 'L.A. Bible'? This isn't about L.A."

The Last Bookstore. DTLA.

See the next page for the L.A. Bible as we imagine it.

THE L.A. BIBLE'S
10 COMMANDMENTS:

#1 @Thou shalt have no other gods except for celebrities and billionaires and hot people.

#2 @Thou shalt not make unto thee any graven image and shall remedy all flaws with body sculpt and Botox.

#3 @Thou shalt not take the name of the Lord thy God Leonardo DiCaprio in vain but may kindly do so to Adrian Grenier if necessary.

#4 @Thou shalt remember the Coachella day to keep it holy.

#5 @Thou shalt honor thy father and thy mother back in Arkansas with photo booth images and mistakes that are hidden in the Hollywood Hills.

#6 @Thou shalt not kill vegans despite the constant temptation.

#7 @Thou shalt not commit adultery and therefore shall stay single until thou art 55 years old and still hit on 22-year-olds (but only if @Thou art rich).

#8 @Thou shalt not work.

#9 @Thou shalt not bear false witness against thy neighbor even if he keeps you up all night listening to EDM and snorting the powder from his broken snow globe.

#10 @Thou shalt not covet the groceries or cars of others but also you can covet things if you need to just don't admit it to your yoga or Al-Anon friends.

ACKNOWLEDGMENTS

Beverly Kessler (for birth), Matthew Margolis, @brooklyncartoons, James Webber, Ned Benson, Steve Grushcow, Fabrice Penot, Allan Loeb, Jonathan Pease, Mercedes Delusive, Maddison Pease, Rose Margolis, Anne Robin, Erica Packer, Emmet Truxes, Maria Caserio and Mario, Mary Kate Glenning, Josh Rudnick, Bridget Berman, her fat dog Kathy, Molly Mandel, Ireland Baldwin, Natasha Bassett, Alex Williamson, Kashmir Snowden-Jones, Kate, Liz Carey, George Nessis, Justin and Megan, Joe and Colter, Julie Hermelin, Todd Lippiatt, Mia Maestro, Cali Bloomgarden, Crosby Tailor, Alfred and Josh, Jen Morrison, David Weiner, Rob Fishman, Chris Paul, Aaron Karp, But Like Maybe, Jordan Santos, The Cartorialist, Dianna Agron, The Yellow Haired Girl, April Henry, Veronique Gabai Pinsky, Neuehouse, Le Labo, Patrick Heij, Marc Webb, Jane Herman, Tim Gallati, David Greenbaum, Max Chow, Sarni Rogers, Mayor Eric Garcetti, Chase Ellman, Josh LeKash, Shauna Falisi, Caroline McKay, Randall Slavin, Matt Phelps, We Are Shadow, Nina Dobrev, CBD Oil, Elana Brooks the best chef in L.A., Megan F, Kacy Hill, Dani Druz, Erewhon, Noah from French Fry, Scott Burns, Brad Rubin, Aui, Kamala Fritzler, Stephanie Delman, Jess Fromm and the entire team at Running Press, Instagram, and the two girls who wouldn't shut the fuck up about Lisa and her "Scchhhwwaaaaagg." But most importantly, thank you to Radley aka The Black Swan (@blackswanstagram).

SUBMISSION CREDITS

#DATING

@iamrickylewis
@lizziehalper
@imalexoliver
@sarahkbartlett +
@booneani
@samijo
@chasewright.ca
@ashleyundrwd
@i.b.profane
@shamikm
@roseguy21
@nickystagram
@emcski
@janewickline
@prettyhipsjefferson
@luckykatypalmer

#SPIRITUALITY

@pamprz
@romeapple
@dougmiddlebrook

@stevnpearl
@chloekarmin
@jessisnotanurse
@jayflats
@sydnyfuruichi
@arielmazal

#FOOD

@lacioffi
@halohaag
@nicole.madsen
@epersk
@taylorleighstyle
@jbinge
@alliereidy
@thischarmingdan
@mariejulian
@bee_gram
@lizglick
@kimhemenway
@natcatwatbat

#HEALTH AND FITNESS

@kyrapellant
@mayaschirn
@livannhines
@alexlarian
@eurube
@rubyrrodriguez
@sagababy
@katyokane
@joseph_reeed
@kirreeves
@kimmy__smalls
@rachelmdavis
@shancarey
@del_compare

#THEYOUTHS

@audrey_marlene
@harry_vaughn
@napoleon_
bonerpants

@itsmemakinna
@claymason
@paigethalia
@saraestefanoss
@curquhartt
@paigero13

#NIGHTLIFE ANDPARTYING

@maddbrown
@oliviacoolins
@shanebaxley
@scottstenholm
@andreaburish
@peytonherzog
@danielglaeser
@druzche
@escmichelle
@captnkurt
@sarahmaymayw
@betsygaghan
@luisbazzlelord_
@connnor.jay
@_anjill_
@tessa_lations
@shaynefalco

#DIGITAL_LIFE

@explora_torrey
@ktrnarymndo
@fraxalato
@kateridion
@cookingforluv
@shmammi
@sheadepmore
@kerridumin
@dropinlate
@instadub92
@gregorycorbett
@taraassi
@meaghanmaples

#ONLY_IN_LA

@washingtonkelly
@hannahraine
@randallslavin
@zurbina
@juju_hrovat
@rtg07
@christinamariestyles
@haleyyjones
@nolanwhitaker
@isabelsstern

@julianamendelsohn
@jeanclaudephoto
@ryanmazie
@danielleraem
@rosswilliamvon
@thatguynamederin
@misslindsaymac
@preilly7

Overheard is a social media brand powered by original, user-generated content. It launched as @OverheardLA on Instagram in late 2015 by L.A. native Jesse Margolis, and it has expanded to include accounts in New York, London, and San Francisco. With content sourced everywhere from hipster cafes, vegan restaurants, nightclubs, and your local goat yoga class, Overheard is the insta-voice of our cities.

@brooklyncartoons is an Instagram account of single-panel cartoons that focuses on the intersection of becoming an adult and the entrenchment of technology in our everyday lives. It is the creation of Emmet Truxes, who in addition to cartooning also runs an L.A.-based architectural and interior design studio. His first book of cartoons, *You Look Better Online*, was published by Abrams in 2017.